AUTHENTIC POWER AND GREATNESS

A Practical Guide to Living an Enlightened Life

AUTHENTIC POWER AND GREATNESS

A PRACTICAL GUIDE TO LIVING AN ENLIGHTENED LIFE

**TIMELESS WISDOM FROM SOME OF THE WORLD'S GREATEST MINDS
TO HELP YOU SUCCEED IN EVERYDAY LIFE AND WORK**

JOSEPH RODARICK LAW

First published in 2019 by New Holland Publishers
London • Sydney • Auckland

Bentinck House, 3–8 Bolsover Street, London W1W 6AB, UK
1/66 Gibbes Street, Chatswood, NSW 2067, Australia
5/39 Woodside Ave, Northcote, Auckland 0627, New Zealand

newhollandpublishers.com

Copyright © 2019 New Holland Publishers
Copyright © 2019 in text: Joseph Rodarick Law
Copyright © 2019 in images:Joseph Rodarick Law

All rights reserved. No part of this publication may be reproduced, stored in a retrieval system or transmitted, in any form or by any means, electronic, mechanical, photocopying, recording or otherwise, without the prior written permission of the publishers and copyright holders.

A record of this book is held at the British Library and the National Library of Australia.

ISBN 9781742579474

Group Managing Director: Fiona Schultz
Publisher: Fiona Schultz
Project Editor: Elise James
Designer: Yolanda La Gorcé
Production Director: Arlene Gippert
Printer: Toppan Leefung Printing Limited

10 9 8 7 6 5 4 3 2 1

Keep up with New Holland Publishers on Facebook
facebook.com/NewHollandPublishers

Testimonials

Here's what some of the world's leading minds are saying about *Authentic Power and Greatness*

"*Authentic Power and Greatness* is a fascinating book packed with wisdom and practical advice."

Honorable Bob Carr
Former Foreign Minister and NSW Premier of Australia

"At Zappos, we focus relentlessly on customer service and delivering happiness to our customers, employees, and vendors. Joseph Law works to enhance the lives of humanity through his organization and through his new book. *Authentic Power and Greatness* has the potential to change the lives of millions."

Tony Hsieh
CEO, Zappos.com

"Joseph is in search of himself. An earnest and sincere student of spiritual life, he adds value to everyone he comes in contact with. He is wise beyond his age. *Authentic Power and Greatness* is an illuminating and easy-to-read book for one's personal and professional lives."

Ashish Chauhan
Managing Director & CEO
Bombay Stock Exchange
(One of top 10 largest stock exchanges in the world)

"*Authentic Power and Greatness* contain timeless wisdom combined with real world practicality for attaining success in one's personal and professional lives. The book is a tribute to all readers who will chart the journey to a new and better tomorrow. Congratulations to Joseph."

Raymond Wong
Film Producer of *"Ip Man"* **series**
(One of the most successful film producers in Hong Kong and China)

"*Authentic Power and Greatness* inspires by reminding us that living an extraordinary life is a path to personal enrichment and the book is a very useful guide for reflecting on where you may be in that journey."

Phil Lynch
Former Managing Director,
Johnson & Johnson Pacific

"*Authentic Power and Greatness* is important reading that will impact all areas of your life, showing you how to create greater success and prosperity in your work, deeper fulfillment in your relationships, and more happiness in your daily experience. This book delivers a message that is inspiring, meaningful and practical."

Marci Shimoff
New York Times bestselling author, *Happy for No Reason and Chicken Soup for the Woman's Soul*

"Rarely have I seen a book so packed with brilliant advice. Reading *Authentic Power and Greatness* is like having a private coaching session with some of the world's most respected thinkers. It's a book I will return to again and again. It's a must-read."

Siimon Reynolds
Multi award winning marketing expert

TESTIMONIALS

"Joseph Law's book *Authentic Power and Greatness* is a wonderful book that sits on my bookshelf amongst my absolute favorites. It is a distillation of timeless wisdom from great minds and I go back to it regularly for inspiration and guidance."

Anh Do
Author, actor, comedian, and artist

"Joseph has shown a real heart to seek out the information that is so easily skimmed over in other books. His passion for human development shines through in his determination to make this book a must-read for anyone who really wants to know what's behind true greatness."

Bessie Bardot
TV and Radio Personality

"*Authentic Power and Greatness* is filled with nuggets of wisdom, gems of inspiration, and treasures from the heart for living your own greatness masterfully. It will inspire millions."

Dr. John Demartini
CEO and Founder of the Demartini Institute

"To make our world a better place, we need more wisdom, more compassion, more love, more kind people and more good books. That's exactly why we need Joseph and his book"

Louis Cheung
Actor and singer-songwriter
Kay Tse
Singer and actress

"If you want to live great or be great in any way (great or small) then you'd best learn from some of the greats. *Authentic Power and Greatness* is a great place to start. You can read in a few minutes what took them a lifetime to learn."

Robert G. Allen
Bestselling author of *The One Minute Millionaire and Multiple Streams of Income*

"In *Authentic Power and Greatness*, Joseph Law brings us out of the dark ages of ego and escorts us into the light of our ever-expanding spiritual expression and creative potential. He frees us from our limiting past and leads us directly into the bright path of our authentic and divinely alive future."

Sonia Choquette
New York Times bestselling author of *Your Heart's Desire*

"A powerful and concise collection from some of the greatest minds in the world that will propel you towards prosperity, success and happiness. I highly recommend."

John R. Burley Educator, Author, Investor

"*Authentic Power and Greatness* is a treasure – every single page is full of inspirational surprises. The wisdom is practical, genuine, and the messages are a must read and live."

Akiane Kramarik
Bestselling author, artist and poet

Contents

Testimonials		5
Acknowledgements		10
Dedication		12
Foreword by Jack Canfield		13
Introduction		16
Chapter 1	Jack Canfield – Bestselling Author	20
	Living a life inspired by purpose	
Chapter 2	Dr. John Demartini – Philosopher	37
	Love and wisdom are the key	
Chapter 3	Marci Shimoff – Happiness Expert	58
	Happiness with effortless ease	
Chapter 4	Fred Alan Wolf – Quantum Physicist	74
	Science with a spiritual twist	
Chapter 5	Bill Bartmann – Billionaire Business Coach	90
	Overcoming adversity and winning the business of life	
Chapter 6	Chin-Ning Chu – Strategist	110
	Ancient Eastern wisdom for today's world	
Chapter 7	Siimon Reynolds – High Achievement Expert	127
	High performance in a demanding world	
Chapter 8	Dr. Edward de Bono – International Leading Thinker	146
	Enhance your thinking power for unstoppable success	
Chapter 9	Sonia Choquette – Professional Life Coach	165
	Unleashing your heart's desire	
Chapter 10	Mingyur Rinpoche – Meditation Master	187
	Meditation demystified and made easy	
About Joseph		206

Acknowledgements

Firstly, I would like to express my deepest gratitude to God for giving me this wonderful opportunity, to serve the lives of humanity. I'm truly humbled by this incredible experience.

Many extraordinary people have shaped me into the person I am today, and this book would not exist without the love, support and friendship of these amazing people.

I extend my deepest gratitude and thanks to these amazing contributing authors (order not in priority): Dr. John Demartini, Marci Shimoff, Fred Alan Wolf, Bill Bartmann, Jack Canfield, Siimon Reynolds, Sonia Choquette, Chin Ning Chu, Mingyur Rinpoche and Dr. Edward de Bono. This book would not have been possible if not for your generous contribution, and it's been my great honor to work with each one of you. I understand that you are all extremely busy people, yet you have been willing to give up your precious time to share your secrets, wisdom, and experiences so that all who read this book may be enriched and enlightened. *Authentic Power and Greatness* is demonstrated by how one's life is lived, and you are all inspirational and shining examples. I salute you all!

My appreciation especially goes to my friend, Jack Canfield, who has lived as such a great role model. Your message, faith, and support are a positive force to help me pursue my path in serving humanity. Jusuf Hariman, my dear friend who I affectionately call my "Uncle" – thank you for guiding, supporting, and loving me throughout the years.

A really big thank you to Fiona Schultz, my brilliant publisher who believed in the message of *Authentic Power and Greatness*. The friendship lasted almost a decade and it is still going strong. Also to the great team at New Holland for

ACKNOWLEDGEMENTS

their amazing support and determination to deliver this book in such a short time. Janet Angelo, Danielle Dorman and Julia Collingwood, you have done a marvelous job working as my editors. Special thanks to CTF for the wonderful concept and cover design. Elaine Chiu, my wonderful assistant and friend, your dedication and unwavering support has made this book possible. John Chan, my graphic designer, you have given yourself generously from day one. I enjoy your humor and treasure our friendship. You are an extraordinary team!

A special thanks to my family for their love, support and understanding. My dearest mum and dad, who have unselfishly devoted their lives so that I may have an opportunity to live my life. My beloved sisters, Shirley and Kathy, your love and unwavering support means a lot to me. I'm incredibly blessed to have you both in my life. I treasure every moment we have spent together in this life journey. I love you all from the bottom of my heart! I am also grateful for the many great teachers from the east and west (Buddha, Lao Tzu, Jesus Christ) whose profound teachings continue to inspire me.

Last but not least, I want to say thank you to so many of my friends who have enriched my life but whom I may have not mentioned here by name, but whom I hold in my heart with great love and gratitude, and to all the great people I have had the wonderful privilege and fortune to meet, on the journey of life. I'm eternally grateful to you all.

Dedication

This book is dedicated with love to the lives of every living person from now to the future. May your life be enriched with inner happiness and greatness.

Foreword

by Jack Canfield

When Joseph first invited me to contribute to his book, Authentic Power and Greatness, I instantly recognized that he was a man on an important mission. This enthusiastic young man has dedicated his life to a higher purpose. He has a sincere and passionate desire to help others and to make the world a better place. Joseph has chosen to follow a higher calling and has committed to using his many gifts in the service of humanity. And now he has written, compiled, and edited an extraordinary collection of writings from some of the brightest and most evolved minds on the planet. As you read this book you will discover that Authentic Power and Greatness is possible for all of us and cannot be measured solely by society's usual standards of success or wealth. Rather, it is demonstrated by how one's life is lived. Like Joseph, I believe a great life is one that is dedicated to love and service, and is inspired by a deep and meaningful purpose, and that contributes to something beyond one's self that adds to the creation of a world founded on love, peace, and joy.

Napoleon Hill, author of *Think and Grow Rich*, wrote, "Every negative event contains within it the seed of an equal or greater benefit." In today's world it seems we are faced with a parade of "negative" events – endless wars, a global economic crisis, rampant social injustice, an epidemic of depression and mental illness, widespread hunger, and an unprecedented destruction of our ecosystem due to global warming. There is certainly a great need for anything that can help us find the "seeds of an equal or greater benefit" that lay within all of these challenging events, and this book does exactly that. It shows us that we can embrace a new paradigm that holds all of these changes and challenges as opportunities for transformation – from living in fear to living in love, from an emphasis on taking to a focus on giving, from a belief in scarcity to a recognition of abundance, from an experience of separation based on distrust and hatred to an experience of inclusion based on trust and tolerance, and from a world filled with despair to a world filled with hope.

Joseph has created a book that teaches the principles of happiness and fulfillment from a holistic perspective, one that includes the integration of family, career, and financial abundance with spiritual growth and a sense of purpose in life. When I first discovered that my personal mission – my true purpose in this life – was "inspiring and empowering people to live their highest vision in the context of love and joy," I chose to devote my life to the fulfillment of that purpose. As a result, I have endeavored to inspire people with stories of courageous men and women who have loved unconditionally, have pursued their dreams with passion, and have overcome huge obstacles with determination and perseverance. And, I have worked tirelessly to empower people with the principles, strategies, techniques, and skills needed to succeed in all areas of life. Joseph has committed himself to the same mission, and the book you now hold in your hands is destined to fulfill this same purpose.

The message of this book is that living a life of greatness is not an experience that is reserved for a privileged few. Joseph and all of the deeply insightful authors in this book are here to tell you that *Authentic Power and Greatness* is possible for every one of us! Joseph has succeeded in making this book accessible to people of all ages and from all backgrounds. He has worked closely with all of the contributors to this book to convey complex spiritual principles and truths in easily understandable and practical ways. *Authentic Power and Greatness* blends the best of success and spiritual principles into a simple, easy-to-read format and compresses years of collective wisdom, knowledge, and experience into potent lessons that have powerful and immediate applications. It also offers brilliant answers to some of the most gripping questions that have ever been asked about life, happiness, and success.

Authentic Power and Greatness contains timeless wisdom in a contemporary package for living a happier, more successful, and more fulfilling life. To live great, you will also need to build the new habits, behaviors, and belief structures that will allow you to create the life you want – and *Authentic Power and Greatness* will show you how to do just that.

Get ready for the read (and the ride) of your life!

Jack Canfield

Co-creator of the *Chicken Soup for the Soul*® series, co-author of *The Success Principles™: How to Get from Where You Are to Where You Want to Be*. Guinness World Record holder for having seven books simultaneously on the *New York Times* Bestseller List.

Introduction

When I was a teenager, there was a natural and almost intense urge to discover my mission and purpose in life. With no true role model to emulate, I began my personal development by reading books in an effort to tap into the knowledge and experience others had attained. I read a few hundred books in my determination to discover the rules to win the game of life. Someday, I would think to myself, when I have achieved enough success, I'll be of service to humanity and help those who are suffering and in need. I was certain that day would come sooner rather than later according to the quick-fix approaches taught in so many of the self-help books I read. For a period of time those success principles worked. However, my journey toward personal fulfillment would be much slower and more gradual, but ultimately, more fulfilling.

In my twenties, I became the general manager of a subsidiary of an investment company whose sales turnover was over a billion dollars. I was always under stress and extremely busy, working seven days a week to stay ahead of the pack at the expense of more important aspects of personal growth such as my health, my family and friends, and my spirituality. Eventually I realized that I wasn't any happier from all the money I made or from attaining the goals I had set for myself on my road to 'success'. I began to sense that my value system was not in alignment with the constant demand of my corporate responsibilities. To get through the demands of the day, I drank a lot of coffee to the detriment of my longer-term health. Although I was doing all the 'right' things, my life actually seemed rather mundane and boring. I felt as though I was going through my daily routine mechanically.

INTRODUCTION

One day I had a realization, an epiphany – a spiritual awakening. I found myself wondering: Is there more to life than getting an education, progressing in your job, raising a family, paying off your home, retiring, and then dying?

These feelings of frustration and dissatisfaction led to a quest for truth. I embarked on a journey of intense inner and outer discovery, through deep meditation, traveling to sacred places in India, learning from many wise teachers, and studying many of the world's traditions (Eastern and Western) in spirituality and wisdom. I began asking myself the same questions that have been asked by philosophers for as long as recorded human history: Who am I? What is my purpose in life? What legacy do I want to leave the world when I depart from this life? Such deep pondering led me through a process of redefining the true nature of success; I no longer thought of it merely as material success. Instead, this new definition of success included the higher principles of living one's purpose, alleviating suffering, and being of service to humanity. I began to realize that personal transformation is a gradual process that does not happen overnight. The path to success is not a destination, but instead is a lifelong journey of commitment.

During this transformative process, I experienced great peace, satisfaction, happiness, and a renewed sense of purpose in life. Then I thought to myself, while many of these ideals, spiritual wisdoms, and higher principles are wonderful, most of them were written thousands of years ago. How can we integrate these timeless wisdoms into the complexities of our modern, everyday lives in practical ways? Many insightful teachers, thinkers, and philosophers have talked about the purpose of life and living a life filled with happiness. The philosopher Aristotle wrote, "Happiness is the meaning and the purpose of life, the whole aim and end of human existence." These ideals seem far off in the distance as we face the complexities of everyday life – bills to pay, a family to raise, health problems to endure, a job we don't like, and on and on it goes, seemingly without end. Obviously, there needs to be a solution for cultivating peace, love, and joy for the modern age without having to sit in a cave meditating for the rest of their lives.

With this in mind, I asked the universe what I could do in my lifetime to serve others and enrich their lives. Through a sequence of what seemed like coincidental events, I was inspired to write this book, Authentic Power and Greatness. I wanted to compile a book that could break down complex, timeless spiritual principles and truths into understandable and practical applications for our modern times. This book, Authentic Power and Greatness, has been written and compiled for that very purpose: to teach the principles of happiness from a holistic perspective, one that includes family, career, spiritual growth, and one's purpose in life. Written in a question-and-answer format through a series of rare and insightful interviews with some of the world's greatest minds, Authentic Power and Greatness will give you private access to the ideas, thoughts, and advice of some of the world's top thinkers in diverse fields.

I had a vision of what I wanted this book to be in its final form, but many things were beyond my control. Through surrendering to the unknown I have been blessed to witness how the compilation of this book has unfolded naturally as it was meant to be. In the process, I have had to overcome many doubts through faith, and in a way, I can look back now with a sense of perspective and see that this was a test of my willingness to live my own purpose in life by following the callings of my heart. I began to embrace the lessons that came my way and I learned that if you want to change the world, it is much easier to start by changing yourself. The process to create this book took much longer than I originally envisioned – almost two years of development with hundreds of hours of accumulated labor. I conducted extensive research about the kind of book I wanted to create and reviewed hundreds of authors, designed over 500 questions with different themes, and interviewed many world-class thinkers and leaders; some of those interviews were through email, some through telephone interviews, some gave their permission to use extracts from their books.

INTRODUCTION

These inspiring men and women have all experienced stress, pain, and confusion, just like every one of us has experienced or is going through right now, yet despite all the setbacks and challenges they've endured, they have found their life's purpose and are living each day with a sense of joy and fulfillment. Authentic Power and Greatness is not a book on theory, but instead is based on the real life experiences of those who have attained mastery over their lives and are now living holistically. There are many challenges and problems in the world today. This book is especially important at this critical time when war, economic downturn, famine, and global warming are rampant and seem to be spreading unabated. The Chinese character for the word 'crisis' consists of two words – the first is the word for crisis and the second is the word for opportunity. This implies that despite whatever crisis we are facing in our circumstances, we always have a choice in life to turn that crisis into an opportunity for new growth, for following a new path, and for carving out true happiness.

I hope that Authentic Power and Greatness can serve as a pathway to help you live an ordinary life in an extraordinary way. This is your birthright, and it is possible for you to attain such a life! Authentic Power and Greatness will not give you all the answers you need, but it will open you to new questions. Through the application of the many principles in this book, you will feel happier, achieve more with less effort, and find deep inner peace without losing your effectiveness in the real world. You will wake up one day to realize you are no longer haunted by a sense of dread but are living a life inspired by purpose. To start Authentic Power and Greatness by living your life's purpose, ponder and embrace this timeless wisdom: "What lies behind you and what lies before you is nothing compared to what lies within you."

Your Friend,

Joseph Rodarick Law

CHAPTER 1

Living a life inspired by purpose

Jack Canfield – Bestselling author

> *I think genuine success comes from discovering what you love to do and finding a way to do it so that it serves yourself and others at the same time.*

Biography

As the beloved originator of the *Chicken Soup for the Soul*® series, Jack Canfield fostered the emergence of inspirational anthologies as a genre – and watched it grow to a billion dollar market. As the driving force behind the development and delivery of over 100 million books sold through the *Chicken Soup for the Soul*® franchise, Jack Canfield is uniquely qualified to talk about success. Behind the empire *Time* magazine called the "publishing phenomenon of the decade" is America's leading expert in creating peak performance for entrepreneurs, corporate leaders, managers, sales professionals, corporate employees, and educators. Affectionately known as "America's #1 Success Coach", Jack has studied and reported on what makes successful people different. He knows what motivates them, what drives them, and what inspires them.

Jack is a Harvard graduate with a Masters Degree in psychological education and one of the earliest champions of "peak-performance", developing the specific methodology and results-oriented activities to help people take on greater challenges and produce breakthrough results.

Mr. Canfield's other best-selling books are – *The Success Principles*™: *How to Get From Where You Are to Where You Want to Be, The Power of Focus, The Aladdin Factor,* and *Dare to Win*. Jack Canfield holds the Guinness World Record for having seven books simultaneously on the *New York Times* Bestseller list – beating Stephen King. He has also been a featured guest on more than 1,000 radio and television programs in nearly every major market worldwide – including *Oprah, 20/20, Inside Edition, The Today Show, Larry King Live, Fox and Friends, The CBS Evening News, The NBC Nightly News, Eye to Eye,* CNN's *Talk Back Live!,* PBS, QVC – many of them on a repeat basis.

How did you start out?

What early experiences shaped the person you are today?

I started my professional career as a history teacher in an all-black inner-city high school in Chicago. Most of my students were not highly motivated, so I quickly became more interested in learning how to inspire them to want to learn and succeed than I was in teaching history. In my quest to find effective motivation techniques, I discovered W. Clement Stone, who was a self-made millionaire worth $600 million. Mr. Stone was a friend of Napoleon Hill, the author of *Think and Grow Rich*, and had started a foundation to teach people his principles of success. Two years later I went to work at the foundation and spent a couple of years teaching those powerful success principles to schoolteachers and counselors as well as businessmen.

I later went back to the university to get a Masters degree in psychological education. I became a psychotherapist, founded the New England Center for Personal and Organizational Development, became a trainer for an international training company, and eventually started my own training company, which I still run today. Along the way I wrote several best-selling books for educators, and a couple for the general public.

The real turning point in my life came when I decided to put all of the inspirational stories I had been sharing in my speeches and workshops into a book, which I eventually co-authored with Mark Victor Hansen. That book was entitled *Chicken Soup for the Soul®*, which – after having been rejected by 144 publishers – went on to sell over 10 million copies worldwide in more than 40 languages. There are now more than 200 books in the series with total sales exceeding 115 million copies.

What do you believe to be the secret of true happiness?

I believe there are several secrets to true happiness. The first is to truly love and accept yourself just the way you are. Most of us have to relearn how to do that. Teaching people how to develop self-esteem has been a huge focus in my work. The next step is to trust yourself: trust your feelings; trust your preferences; trust you intuition. Finally, you have to learn to trust the universe and to have faith that everything is unfolding as it should.

Another major key to happiness is learning to take 100 percent responsibility for everything that happens in your life. That means giving up all blaming and complaining about how the world is. It's coming to grips with the idea that you are indeed the one who is creating your reality by the thoughts you think, the images you hold in your mind, the feelings you feel, the choices you make and the actions you do or don't take. Once you truly get this, you can begin to create the life you want through intentionally using the power of your mind.

Along these same lines, we have to be willing to let go of our judgments about how other people should be. Most of our pain comes from trying to control things we have no control over and from believing that other people and conditions should be different than they are. When you give up judging and trying to control others, and focus instead on creating what you want for yourself, you find an inner peace from which you can more effortlessly create your life as you'd like it to be.

How would you define genuine success?

I think genuine success comes from discovering what you love to do and finding a way to do it so that it serves yourself and others at the same time. Every one of us was born with a set of unique talents and abilities. We have inborn preferences and natural styles that we need to honor. Some of us are natural leaders; others are happier in support roles. Some are natural salespeople; others are born to be creative in the arts. The trick is to pursue your greatest interests. When you discover your true purpose and develop a vehicle through which you can express it, you will experience a great sense of success. And if you can find a way to make money doing it at the same time, then all the better.

For me, success is having the ability to create the conditions that allow me to do all of the things I love in every area of my life. I have created a staff, colleagues, offices, the infrastructure, the financial resources, and the time I need to pursue my professional interests and make a huge difference in the world. I have created the family structure and the friends I need to enjoy loving and fulfilling relationships. I have created the time and the resources I need to keep my body nourished, healthy, and fit. I have created the resources I need to surround myself with beautiful art, furniture, and music. I have created the resources and contacts I need to travel comfortably to any place in the world that I want to visit. I have the time and the money to pursue any educational and personal development experience that I want to explore.

What do you believe have been the best-kept secrets to your success?

I think the secrets to my success have been four-fold.

First, I always listened to my inner guidance. I listened to what I was interested in and pursued it with all of my heart and soul. I was always willing to let go of where I was – literally and figuratively – in order to follow my dreams. By the time I was 39 I had lived in nine states, attended three universities, built three businesses, taken more than 100 workshops, read over 1,000 books, and listened to more audio programs than I can count. I have always been a voracious learner, and by honoring my desire to increase my own self-awareness, I also discovered ways to help others be more successful in every area of their lives.

Second, I was willing to work hard. Because I was passionate about my work. I worked long hours, approached every task with excellence, and devoted myself to never-ending improvement in every area of my work and my life.

Third, I learned early on that life is a team sport. I always surrounded myself with partners, co-authors, and great staff with whom I shared generously.

Fourth, I have always sincerely cared about the people I serve – sometimes to a fault. But I truly love people, and I love how I feel when I watch them wake up and successfully apply the principles and strategies I have taught them. I love what I do, and I love the people for whom I do it.

You have said that meditation is an important key to happiness. How has meditation affected your life?

Yes, one of the keys to happiness and peace of mind for me is a regular meditation practice. Through meditation, I am able to reconnect to God, Source and Infinite Intelligence. As I surrender to that which emerges during meditation, I find that my emotions are calmer, my awareness is deeper, my choices are wiser, my actions are more effective, my body is healthier, my mind is less stressed, and my life on the whole is more meaningful.

What is the true meaning of "living on purpose"?

I think we are all born with a deep and meaningful purpose that we have to discover. Your purpose is not something you need to make up; it's already there. You just have to uncover it. You can begin to discover your purpose by exploring two things: 1) What do you love to do? What makes you happy? and 2) What comes easy to you?

Of course, it takes work to develop your talents – even the most gifted musician still has to practice – but it should feel natural, like rowing downstream rather than upstream. I love to teach, to write, to coach, to facilitate, to train, and to develop transformational seminars, workshops, and courses. I love to bring other leaders together for conferences and to co-create new approaches to our work.

These things come easy for me. Although I invested many years in learning how to master these skills, I loved every minute of it. In other words, work is required, but suffering is not. If you are struggling and suffering, you are probably not living on purpose.

What advice would you give to someone who is still searching for their purpose?

Let me share with you a quick little exercise from my book *The Success Principles* that may help you discover your purpose.

First, ask yourself, *What are two qualities I most enjoy expressing in the world?* Mine are *love* and *joy*.

Second, ask yourself, What are two ways I most enjoy expressing these qualities? Mine are inspiring and empowering people. I inspire people with the moving stories that I tell in my seminars and that I write about in my books, and I empower them by teaching them powerful success strategies that they can apply in their own lives

Once you've answered these questions, take a few moments and write a description of what the world would look like if it were operating perfectly according to you. In my perfect world, everybody is living their highest vision where they are doing, being, and having everything they want. Finally, combine all three of the above into one statement, and you will have a clear idea of your purpose. Mine is "inspiring and empowering people to live their highest vision in a context of love and joy."

Can you give us a real life example of how we can start "living on purpose"?

One of my Platinum Master Mind coaching students, Dr. Sudheer Gogte, a successful cardiologist, was struggling to identify his purpose. I suggested another exercise from my book, and asked him to look back over his life and answer the question, *When have I felt most fulfilled?*

He shared three periods in which he felt the happiest and most fulfilled. First, he told me about a time with his grandfather when he was growing up in India. The second was his experience of playing with his own grandchildren. The third was a time he spent vacationing on a sailboat. When I asked him what was common to all three of these experiences, he told me that it was the sense of freedom that he felt.

Noticing that none of his three experiences related to his profession in medicine, I asked him to tell me about his most fulfilling experiences as a doctor. The incidences he reported were when he had donated his services for free or for a lesser fee than his partners thought he should have charged. He shared about a time when he took a much longer time than usual during an office visit to support and encourage a family who were in fear of losing their father during an impending heart surgery. As we examined his life further, it became apparent that he took very little time for himself. He was always on call, always working late, always overscheduled with little or no free time for self-care. I asked him why this was so. He answered that people could die if he didn't attend to them. The problem became clear: By attending only to his patients and never to himself, he was – in a sense – dying.

To drive this point home, I asked Sudheer what he would do in the following situation: "A patient comes to you for an operation. If you operate on this patient, you will die. If you don't operate on him, he will die. It's him or you. What would you do?" He reflected quietly on this scenario for a long time, and then finally he said, "I would choose to live, rather than die myself. It doesn't make sense to kill myself to save others." This was a turning point in his life. He later told me that while he still wants to serve people, he now knows he has a right to take care of himself – his mind, his body, and his needs. This cardiologist now places a higher value on doing what truly comes from his heart, not someone else's.

From these two exercises he crafted the following life purpose statement: *To bring joy, compassion, happiness, and freedom to people in the world and experience the same for myself while doing it.*

In your view, how can we create a life with more meaning and joy?

My answer to this question is simple: Find a way to serve.

Back in 2004 I was honored by the Academy of Achievement for having made a significant contribution to the world. One of the previous recipients who spoke at that event was Ken Behring, the author of *Road to Purpose: One Man's Journey Bringing Hope to Millions and Finding Purpose Along the Way*. He was a worth about $500 million dollars. During his speech, he told us that his life had gone through four stages. The first stage was about "Stuff." He thought that if he had the right stuff he'd be happy. So he bought the houses, the cars, the boat, the airplane – all of the usual toys – and yet, he was not happy.

He described the second stage of his life as the acquisition of "Better Stuff." He thought he'd be happier if he had a better house, a better car, a bigger airplane, and so on. So he bought them. But he still wasn't happy. Then he figured that maybe he had focused on the wrong stuff, so he embarked on the third stage of his life, which he called "Different Stuff." This is when he joined with a partner and bought the Seattle Seahawks. He thought for sure that if he was the co-owner of a professional football team, he would be happy. But he wasn't. What to do?

It was at this time that a friend invited Ken to join him on his private jet to fly to Europe and hand out wheelchairs to kids who had been born without limbs or who had lost their legs as a result of having stepped on a landmine. Ken accepted the invitation. He said that bringing hope and freedom to these children made him truly happy for the first time in his life. When he returned home, he started the Wheelchair Foundation, which has now given away more than 750,000 wheelchairs to children and adults all over the world.

Ken told us about one of his early trips to give away wheelchairs, when he picked up an eleven-year-old boy in Mexico and gently set him down in a wheelchair. When he went to leave and get another wheelchair for one of the other children, the boy wouldn't let go of his leg. When Ken turned back around to face him, the boy said through his tears, "Please don't leave yet. I want to memorize your face, so when we meet again in heaven, I can thank you one more time." Ken said at that moment he experienced pure joy. He later told us, "When I see the happiness in the eyes of the people who get a wheelchair, I feel that this is the greatest thing I have ever achieved in my life." Contributing to others is the fastest way I know to infuse your life with authentic love and joy.

How can we identify our life's mission, and why is it important to do so?

I believe that mission and vision should flow from life purpose. While purpose is inborn, I believe we get to choose how we want to express that purpose in the world. What do we hope to accomplish in the fulfillment of that purpose? Through what vehicle and in what form do we wish to channel our purpose? I teach that a mission is something that can never be fulfilled. Rather, it is a more general statement about the contribution you are committed to making in the world. On the other hand, one's vision is more concrete. It is stated in measurable terms.

Can you give us an example by sharing your vision statement?

How do you keep track of it?

Here is my vision statement:

To positively impact one billion lives through inspirational and empowering print, radio, TV, movies, products, speeches, seminars, training and philanthropy.

To inspire and empower people – including my staff – to live their highest vision of life in a context of love and joy by providing quality products and services (including stories, books, audio and video programs, speeches, seminars, training, coaching, and consulting) delivered with love, joy, integrity, and excellence. We do that by focusing on stories, principles and techniques that expand awareness, increase love, reduce hatred and intolerance, build self-esteem and self-confidence, enhance self-expression, improve relationships, foster cooperation, enhance peak performance, and empower individuals, groups, and organizations to achieve their dreams and goals.

In terms of tracking my purpose, I know I am well on my way to fulfilling this mission and vision because my books have already reached more than 150 million people, my appearances on *Oprah*, *Larry King*, *Montel*, the *Today* show and two PBS specials have reached another 50 million people, and – through my role in the movie *The Secret* – I've reached over 60 million more. Just this past year, Anhui Publishing Company in China has contracted to publish almost every *Chicken Soup for the Soul* book in Chinese and in English, including a special edition for schools with Chinese on one page and English on the facing page that will be used as a textbook to teach English as a second language. This development alone holds the potential to reach another 500 million people just in China!

Why do we feel the happiest and most fulfilled when we commit to our life's purpose?

Because when we are aligned with our life purpose, we are deeply connected to our unique genius. We are doing what we are here to do and playing the role that we were born to play.

I have come to understand that every one of us was born with an infallible way to know what is for our highest good. We just have to tune into what we are feeling, and if we are not feeling love, joy, peace, and ease, this is nature's way of telling us that we are off course.

How can we find out what is good for us and make great decisions?

This is so counter to the way most of us in the West were educated that it's hard for many of us to align with this notion, but it has always proven to be true in my life. Whenever I am following my joy, pursuing that which I am passionate about, I have been successful. Whenever I was doing something only because I thought I should or because I thought it would earn lots of money, it was never as successful.

What is the "Law of Attraction"?

I wrote a whole book about this entitled Jack Canfield's *Key to Living the Law of Attraction*. In it I explain that the Law of Attraction is the most powerful law in the universe. And, just like gravity, it is always operating whether you are aware of it or not. Simply put, the Law of Attraction says that you will attract into your life whatever you focus on. Whatever you give your energy and attention to will be magnetized to you. This means whatever you think about, talk about, read about, watch on television, listen to on the radio, worry about, fantasize about, and feel strongly about, you will attract more of into your life. Therefore, if you stay focused on all the good and positive things in your life, you will automatically draw to yourself more good and positive things. Likewise, if you focus on lack and negativity, then that is what you will draw to yourself.

How can we use the "Law of Attraction" to enhance our lives?

The key to utilizing the Law of Attraction is to constantly focus on, talk about, visualize and expect to receive that which you want – not what you don't want. To use this Law to your benefit, you have to quit talking about your unwanted current reality and do two things instead: 1) appreciate and celebrate that which you already have; and 2) focus on, talk about, believe, visualize, affirm, and expect that all you desire is already on its way to you. Maintain a constant focus on your vision. Keep your eye and your conversation on what you are already grateful for and what you are creating.

What are the steps to activating the "Law of Attraction"?

Take time to clarify exactly what you want in every area of your life without limiting yourself by worrying about how you are going to get it. Then write a vivid and complete "ideal scene" of what it will look, sounds, and feel like when you actually have it. Do this for every aspect of your ideal vision – job and career, finances, health and fitness, relationships, fun and recreation, possessions, personal and spiritual growth, and the contribution you want to make to the world.

Next, create a vision board – either in the form of a vision book or a screen saver – that contains visual images of your vision already manifested. Take time every day to close your eyes and visualize each ideal scene as already complete, and, most importantly, to feel the feelings you would feel if you had already achieved this goal or desire.

Next, release your request to the universe. Trust that you are now attracting the ideas, people, resources, money, and opportunities that you need to fulfill every aspect of your vision. Relax, and trust that the timing will be perfect. Believe that it is happening, and look for evidence that supports your belief that what you desire is on its way. You'll notice inspirations, ideas and opportunities will start coming into your awareness. Pay attention to them.

The next step is to begin taking action on the creative impulses you receive. There are two kinds of action – obvious actions and inspired actions. For example, if you want to be a doctor, the obvious actions are to study anatomy, biology, and biochemistry, apply to medical school, and so on. Inspired actions, on the other hand, arise from your intuition, during meditation, or occur to you as sudden impulses that have a deep feeling of rightness to them. An example might be that one afternoon you get this overwhelming urge to take some cookies to the elderly woman who lives down the street who always treated you kindly when you were a kid, so you do. When she invites you into her house, she introduces you to her nephew who is visiting, and he turns out to be the Dean of the Harvard Medical School.

Finally, to fully utilize the Law of Attraction in your life, you have to become a vibrational match with whatever it is you want to attract into your life. This means creating and maintaining an emotional state that matches the one you will experience when you actually get the thing you are focusing on. If your goal is to be rich, you need to focus on feeling abundant now. You can do this by appreciating what you already have, and continually finding more and more things to be grateful for. You can do it by being generous with what you already have. Most importantly, you do it by thinking abundant thoughts and feeling rich right now.

If your desire is to attract your soul mate into your life, start feeling happy about the relationships that you already enjoy. Act as if you are already loved and adored. Pamper yourself. Buy yourself flowers. Clean up your house or apartment the way you would if you were expecting company. Bring closure to your past relationships by forgiving any hurts and appreciating all the good things that you experienced. Let go of any resentments, guilt, or hurt you might be carrying from the past. Find appreciation for the lessons you've learned from previous lovers so that you can be free of the past and live in a genuine state of positive excitement about the future.

What significant quotes or words of wisdom most inspire you?

"I am only a pencil in the hand of God." – Mother Teresa

"I am always doing that which I cannot do in order to learn how to do it." – Pablo Picasso

Many people would like to make a difference in the world. Where can they begin?

My advice is to start right where you are. One of my all-time favorite quotes speaks directly to this point:

"To reject fear and to respond with inspiration, strength, hope, and imagination . . . the work remains in essence what it has always been; to love, to connect, to serve, to care, and to stand for and create wholeness in every way we can." – David Spangler

CHAPTER 2

Love and wisdom are the key

Dr. John Demartini – Philosopher

> Love of self is also a prerequisite to loving others. They actually go hand in hand.

Biography

Dr. John Demartini is a human behavioral specialist, educator, author, and founder of the Demartini Institute, a private research and education institute with a focus on empowering individuals and organizations and transforming micro and macro social dynamics. His scope of knowledge and experience is a culmination of 36 years of research and studies of more than 28,000 texts covering over 200 different disciplines ranging from psychology, philosophy, metaphysics, theology, neurology, and physiology. He has written over 40 books and some of his bestselling titles include *The Breakthrough Experience – a Revolutionary New Approach to Personal Transformation, Count Your Blessings, How to Make One Hell of a Profit and Still Get to Heaven, Heart of Love, You Can Have an Amazing Life in Just 60 Days, The Riches Within, The Gratitude Effect* and recently *From Stress to Success*.

Born in Houston Texas, Dr. Demartini was one of two children. At the age of seven he was told he had a learning disability and would never read, write, or communicate. At fourteen he was a high school dropout living on the streets and panhandling for food to survive. After a near-death experience at seventeen, due to strychnine poisoning, Dr. Demartini made a decision that would change his life forever. He decided to become a teacher, healer, and philosopher who traveled the world.

Today, as a presenter, Dr. Demartini has shared the stage with such noted speakers as Stephen Covey, Dr. Donald Beck, Les Brown, Mark Victor Hansen, Deepak Chopra, Wayne Dyer, Dr. Patch Adams and many others. He has been a welcomed guest on over 3,000 radio and television talk shows including CNN's *Larry King Live* and CBS's *The Early Show*. Dr. Demartini was also one of the featured philosopher/teachers in the world-renowned hit movie, *The Secret*. He is considered foremost in the field of human behavior, philosophy, and personal transformation. Dr Demartini is dedicated to expanding human awareness and potential in all markets and social sectors and travels over 360 days a year to over 56 countries to share his research and findings across the globe. Dr Demartini is the originator of The Demartini Method®, a revolutionary new tool in human transformation and empowerment that is being used by many psychologists, professional and personal coaches, social workers, and health professionals across the world.

He has offices in Houston, Texas, at the Williams Tower, 52nd floor, and maintains his residence on The World, the only resort community to continually circumnavigate the globe.

How did you start out? What early experiences shaped the person you are today?

At the age of seventeen, I met an inspired man named Paul C. Bragg who assisted me in awakening to a vision of being a teacher, healer, and philosopher. He helped me discover my inspiring life mission and a vision of what my life could be if I cultivated a belief in what is possible for myself.

At the age of eighteen, after years of struggling with learning difficulties, I had the opportunity to read Gottfried W. Leibniz's *Discourse on Metaphysics*. It was through this philosophical book that I was introduced to what he called the "divine order". He believed that few individuals ever got a glimpse of this universal magnificence but for those who did their lives were changed forever. This inspiring concept brought tears to my eyes and became the subject of 36 years of research in order to further understand this hidden order for myself and to assist others in discovering it too.

So began my quest to discover all I could about universal laws and all aspects of human behavior, especially in the area of human potential and healing. I believe that through dedication to my vision, and persisting through both the pains and pleasures of the journey, I have created the inspiring opportunities that I get to experience across the world today.

What do you believe is the best way for a person to find their purpose in life?

Take the time to determine what you truly value most in life and live your life accordingly. When you live congruently with your highest values, your life will flow with greater synchronicity and meaning.

You will feel more fulfilled, inspired and purposeful. Achievements will come to you in seemingly effortless ways because you will be doing what you love to do and loving what you do.

In many of my books, I share what I call the Demartini Method of Value Determination™. Through this method you can determine what is truly most important, what your highest priority is, or what you value most, which is the inspiring essence underlying your purpose. At any given point in your life, the answer to the question, 'What is my purpose in life?' is literally demonstrated in the things you do, the topics you speak about, the way you spend your time and energy and in the manner in which you live – in essence what you value most. By asking yourself very specific value-determining questions, you can gain insight into what is truly most important to you. This is the key to structuring your life in a way that will bring you meaning and fulfillment and, when infused into your vocational service, will give you an inspired purpose for living.

What do you believe to be the secret to true happiness?

Give up searching for happiness and appreciate all the things you have right now. Beyond the fleeting emotion that some call "happiness" exist the lasting and deeply fulfilling feelings of gratitude and love. True fulfillment comes with the recognition that life is magnificent just the way it is at that moment. That there is and always will be a balance between up and down, good and bad, happy and sad. When you love and appreciate the world the way it is, and embrace the balance of complementary opposites that life offers you, you are given more to feel love and appreciation for.

How do you define genuine success?

Genuine success, or what I prefer to term fulfillment, is the result of setting goals and objectives that are truly congruent with your true highest values and living in a state of appreciation for what life offers along the journey. Whether you are barefoot and living on a beach or surrounded with all the extras that often accompany wealth, you are truly successful when you know your life is in line with your vision of what "success" means to you. Comparing yourself to others who you imagine to be, do or have more than you will probably distract yourself from your own achievement of success.

How can we develop more clarity in our vision?

The quality of your life is based upon the quality of the questions you ask yourself. If you are looking to develop more clarity in your vision, it is wise to ask yourself the questions that will enable you to do exactly that. The key to these questions is to be specific and probe as deeply as possible into what you would truly love to fulfill in every area of you life so that you get to the heart of your vision. Start with the answers and details that you do know with certainty and keep asking what else specifically you would love to fulfill. Read it and refine it, over and over again, until you are certain and inspired. Make sure there is congruency between your vision and your highest values and between the different components of your vision. Make sure that one aspect of your vision is not contradicting another. Your vitality in life will be directly proportionate to the vividness and congruency of your vision.

What is the "hierarchy of values" and why is that important?

In simple terms, your "hierarchy of values" is a list of what your highest to lowest priorities are; in other words, the things you value most to least in life. To support people in clarifying their hierarchy, I have developed a series of twelve questions (the Demartini Method of Value Determination™), the answers to which allow you to see what you value most based upon what your life is demonstrating. You may believe that you value one thing more than another, but your life itself is the true demonstration of what you actually value.

Your highest values will tend to express themselves in one or many of seven areas of your life: *spiritual, mental, vocational, financial, familial, social,* and *physical*. In my experience, about 75 percent of men tend to value mental, financial, and vocational, while about 75 percent of women tend to focus on familial, social, and physical beauty. Roughly twenty-five percent of men focus on the areas more common to women, and vice versa.

Sometimes you may allow your fears to keep you from living consciously according to your priorities, convincing yourself that you do not know what you would love to do in life. Once you break through those fears you go on to create a more inspired and authentic life, where you love what you do and do what you love. Such fears are broken through by asking the right questions, which balance your perceptions.

Why do we need to align our values with our goals?

The areas you value most are the areas where you live with the greatest level of focus, discipline, reliability, enthusiasm, and energy. Any time you set goals that align with your highest values, you increase the probability of you achieving them, because you are most creative and persistent in the areas that inspire you most.

How important is our self-image to our lives? How can we improve our self-image?

Ultimately, you receive exactly what you feel you deserve, no more and no less. The outer world is a reflection of your inner world. When you raise your sense of self-worth you allow yourself to receive more, set bigger goals and generally expand your awareness and influence in all areas of your life. When you value yourself, the world values you. It's that simple.

Why do we need to develop a life master plan and how does one develop such a plan?

You become a master of achievement when you plan and focus on ever-finer details of what you truly would love to fulfill. If you can see your desired outcome in your mind in perfect detail before you take action, you are infinitely more likely to achieve it. Similarly, if you do not have a cause greater than the immediate needs of yourself, you are more likely to find it difficult to rise beyond yourself. The greater your cause, the greater your potential achievement and wealth. More people will want to support your cause, be a part of it, and invest in it when you are certain and clear.

One of the secrets of building greater wealth and managing money wisely is making sure you have a great cause to which money can flow. You won't find any person of great wealth, or any great foundation of wealth, without it being built upon a great cause. Make sure you have a cause and a masterfully designed plan. Remember that when you fail to plan, you plan to fail and when you take the time to set out the details of what dreams you would love to fulfill you are way more likely to achieve them or succeed.

Do you have any advice for staying on track and retaining momentum in the achievement of one's goals?

Ensure that your goals are congruent with your highest values and you will be more likely to stay on track and build momentum. Also, ensure the goals you set are realizable and based upon stable and steady ground, for the higher your expectation the greater your letdown can become when they are not. This is not to say that great expectations are not healthy. They can be. But they must be backed up with firm planning, strategies, and methodical actions. Work through any possible obstacles that might arise in advance. Guidance or mentorship from someone who has already been there or done what you would love to fulfill is wise. The more details that you plan the less likely you are to run into obstacles and the more you are likely to achieve.

What are visualization and affirmation?

What you see for yourself and what you say to yourself are two powerful ingredients in shaping who you are as a person and what you will achieve or fulfill in the world. Visualization and affirmations are therefore helpful tools in allowing you to take control of shaping your own reality. They are powerful achievement and success tools that have been used since the beginning of human history in all areas of life. Clear, congruent visions and concise, inspiring statements can bring you amazing results.

What is the biggest obstacle to manifesting what we want?

You stand in the way of your own success when you set goals that are incongruent with your true higher values and have unrealistic expectations in terms of what you want and when. Either adjust your goals to match your values or adjust your values to match your goals. Otherwise unrealistic expectations can lead to frustrating results and volatile emotions.

What are the seven common fears that stop us from going after our dreams and visions?

There are seven basic fears that can run your life and keep you from achieving the things you desire most:

1. Fear of breaking the morals or ethics of some perceived spiritual authority.
   (I don't want to be considered a bad person or go to hell.)

2. Fear of not having enough mental capability.
   (I'm not smart enough. I don't have the credentials or degree.)

3. Fear of failure. *(I'll fall short. I may not achieve.)*

4. Fear of losing or not making money.
   (I'll go broke or bankrupt. I won't make enough money to survive.)

5. Fear of losing loved ones.
   (My parents might disown me, my lover will leave me, or my kids will hate me ...)

6. Fear of societal rejection. *(I'm afraid of what everyone will think, I won't fit in, and people won't want to be with me.)*

7. Fear of not having physical capability. *(I'm not tall enough, strong enough, or good-looking enough. I don't have the energy for all this.)*

Why is inner balance important and how can we attain it?

The definition of inner balance is not just about working out a way of balancing your daily or weekly time, focus, and activities in the key areas of life, but it is also about appreciating the intrinsic balance of opposites that exist both within yourself and in the world around you. To create such an inner balanced state, it is wise to find your center, by asking questions that shift the way you perceive your daily experiences. For example: "losing a job" can bring with it just as many benefits as drawbacks. It may initiate actions toward a long-sought goal of innovative entrepreneurship. To focus on only the loss, without the accompanying opportunities will result in lopsided emotions and inertia. To appreciate both sides of the equation simultaneously will create inner balance and gratitude for what opportunities actually exist.

How should we allocate our energy and time on a daily and weekly basis?

By aligning your long-term goals with your highest values, by prioritizing your short-term objectives and by using a 'to-do checklist' for your daily actions you can vitalize your energy and accomplish amazing results. Creating either a hard copy or computerized daily checklist that includes actions that can be prioritized has proven to work wonders. Simply write out all the action steps that have proven to maximize your accomplishment each day and check them off as they are being completed throughout the day. When you work from ABCs instead of XYZs you elevate your self-worth. By also creating prioritized daily delegations lists you help clarify for others what they are to do. Being more concise through clear writing and by giving others your priorities you ensure that your most important delegated actions get done. When you don't prioritize your delegated tasks, your employees tend to do the easiest things first, and possibly the most important things last – or sometimes not at all. As long as they get the highest priority actions accomplished, even if they don't get the whole list completed, at least the most important items get completed.

What is the distinction between "heart" and "mind"?

When you speak congruently and with a balanced perspective, both your mind and heart come into action. Your mind, though intellectual, without an accompanying heart, leaves something missing in its message. But when you intelligently speak gratefully through your heart, your words flow smoothly and you communicate what inspires you from deep within your heart to others and impact them as well as harmonize your own life.

When your head and your heart are not in sync, not only does your body feel stressed and unhealthy, but your life reflects such lack of ease. The secret is living congruently, where your actions, thoughts and feelings work together and create a sense of effortlessness. The key is to speak and live intelligently from your heart.

How can we improve our communications skills?

Certain individuals just seem to know how to speak straight from the heart and communicate effectively with others. They're able to move people to work together; respect one another; and take powerful, collaborative action. Some of these insightful, inspiring men and women become leaders of significant societal movements or the heads of major companies, while others have less public influence and do their magic in the realms of community, family, friendships, and romantic partnerships. The secret of these individuals' success is that they communicate with others in terms of their highest values. They link the message they are communicating with what is most important to that individual and / or group. The key to maximizing your communication skills is therefore to take the time to understand your audience and genuinely seek to find ways to link your most inspiring message with their highest values. When you do, magical relationships occur.

Why is it important to be in a state of gratitude, and how can we cultivate this state?

Operating from a state of appreciation or gratitude is not only the secret to fulfillment, but it's also the secret to decreasing the editing, distractions and wanderings in life. You have more vitality when you are grateful for all that you are, all that you do, and all that you have. Every single day, stop, reflect and think about what you could be grateful for. Make it your aim to be appreciative of your life. Acknowledge the magnificence that you experience.

It has been said that forgiveness is one of the greatest healers. Do you believe this is true and, if so, why?

The supposed need for forgiveness is actually based upon an incomplete awareness, or a somewhat self-righteous illusion, that makes someone else bad or wrong and then presumes, through judging and pardoning, their verdict and release. Apology is also unwisely judging yourself in the same illusive manner, and both forgiveness and apology are guaranteed to perpetuate the presence of whatever it is you judge. The only thing that transcends these illusory dynamics is true and complete awareness and love. Ultimately there is nothing to forgive in this universe, nor anything to apologize for. Whenever someone does something to you, it is wiser to ask yourself have you done the same or similar thing, and how has it served you. Just keep asking these two questions until the initially charged emotion subsides. This calms down the judgment and allows your heart to re-open to the truth of the hidden order and ever presence of love.

How can one's heart be opened to allow more peace and love?

Love of self is also a prerequisite to loving others. They actually go hand in hand. Everything you see in others is a reflection of what actually exists within you, though you may be too humble or too proud to admit it. If you love yourself for all that you are; you are more likely to love others for all that they are because you lift your projected conditions and expectations. You recognize that each individual displays all the many human traits in their own way. Any trait that exists serves in some way or else it would have become extinct. It is not what happens to you as much as it is your perceptions.

Love is all there is. Love is a synthesis of complementary opposites. It includes peace and war, good and bad, up and down, happy and sad, and all others pairs of opposites. We live in a world of chaos and order and both make up a universal form of love. When we appreciate this balanced truth and become grateful for all that is and all that is not, our minds become balanced and our hearts essentially open to the fullness of life.

How can we raise our self-esteem and confidence?

By focusing on the areas of your life where you are already confident you further raise your self-image. You are already confident somewhere in your life yet you may be minimizing where this is as a result of comparisons you have made about others and unrealistic expectations you have imposed upon yourself. Your areas of confidence are those most aligned to your highest values. When we acknowledge the areas in which we are confident, you let go of the illusion of lack and have more energy to focus on developing our ever-present strengths.

What is synchronicity?

When opportunity meets preparation. When you are living according to your highest values and focused on your most inspiring goals, the universe seems to clear a path of action and bring to you the people, places, things, ideas, or events you require to fulfill your mission and achieve your vision. Synchronicity is also revealed through the ever-changing blend of complementary opposites that simultaneously occur throughout each day.

Do you believe that every setback and obstacle is a blessing in disguise? If so, why?

Bruce Lee became the world's greatest martial artist because, after being beaten in the streets of Hong Kong as a young man he swore he would not let it happen again. Ray Charles, Stevie Wonder, and Jose Feliciano turned blindness into musical genius. Paul Bragg nearly died of lung disease and as a result, created health-food stores and became the world's foremost proponent of the breath and health of life. The great director Martin Scorsese had asthma as a child and was kept in an attic room where he watched the world go by through a tiny window, like a camera lens, and to pass the time, he imagined stories about the people below. Nelson Mandela was imprisoned for 28 years and used that time to develop his wisdom and understanding so that he became a symbol for freedom and racial harmony, emerging as the leader of his entire nation.

Benefits and drawbacks, or positives and negatives, remain ever perfectly balanced. The further down and out you have been the further up and in you can go. The early lives of the great masters are characterized by much challenge and so-called hardship. That is where they unveiled their power to achieve what they did. Their voids became their values and the challenges became their opportunities.

What are the secrets to healing on physical, emotional, mental and spiritual levels?

Gratitude and love are the two greatest wellness promoters in life. You will not find anything more powerful than these two heart-opening healers. In order to heal any part of your life you can shift your focus onto what you can be grateful for in any area of your life. Anything you cannot say thank you for in life will run your life symptomatically down until you do.

When you experience the imbalanced emotional states called fear and guilt, you produce disease. That is the beauty and magnificence of the body. Your body is doing whatever it can to show you where you have imbalanced your perceptions. Your body is giving you feedback, with every sign and symptom, about where you're lying about life's equilibrium and seeing imbalance. Disease isn't terrible; it is an essential guide. The mind-body connection works together in order to assist you to grow in your quest for and understanding of the truth of love.

How can we best cope with stress in modern life and attain balance?

Stress is a sign that you are attempting to live according to someone else's values and / or priorities, rather than your own. When what you are doing is linked to your highest values you are less likely to feel stressed. When you are doing what you love to do and loving what you do, what is there to have to balance? Stress is the inability to adapt to a changing environment. When you are rigid in your views, judge unwisely and hold on to unrealistic expectations toward yourself or others, you become stressed more easily.

To rejuvenate the body and mind, why is it important to set aside quiet time every day?

Some of the greatest accomplishments of human genius have been birthed during contemplative moments of silence. This is the value of meditation, which is often misunderstood as some complicated or difficult ritual. It can be that, too, but it can also be as simple as spending some time, however brief, in quietude to allow your mind to stop fussing over trivialities. You can do this sitting up, or even lying down, before or after dinner or lunch. It's vital to find time for such meditation or contemplation, a time when you simply remain in pure silence, without saying a word. Silent meditation heals and reveals.

Are making money and the pursuit of spirituality incompatible?

Spirit requires matter to express itself, and matter needs spirit to give it motion and meaning. Some of the biggest religions that exist today are also the wealthiest in terms of assets and liquid capital from donations or acquisitions.

Some people make arbitrary distinctions between spirit and matter, but you might ask: Where do you not find God or the spirit? You may see someone meditating or praying and think, 'That's a spiritual activity,' and then see someone else exchanging money to make a purchase and think, 'Well, that's obviously a material activity.' And yet the meditator may be praying for personal gain, while the shopper may be joyously buying a gift for a loved one. If you knew what was really occurring, you might completely reverse your first opinions.

If you deeply investigate what you call material actions, you might find that they're spiritual in essence. If you investigate what you think of as spiritual, you may discover that it involves material objectives. Spirit and matter are not at odds with each other, they are inseparable.

What are the seven treasures that are hidden within every person?

1. Inspiration & Truth – Your Spiritual Treasures
2. Creativity & Genius – Your Mental Treasures
3. Achievement & Service – Your Vocational Treasures
4. Wealth & Contribution – Your Financial Treasures
5. Love & Intimacy – Your Familial Treasures
6. Power & Leadership – Your Social Treasures
7. Vitality & Strength – Your Physical Treasures

Can you recommend some tools and techniques to help better organize one's life?

Read books on the subject and take every opportunity to associate yourself with people who assist you in being accountable to your mission and vision in life. When you surround yourself with the right people, places, and resources of information you are more likely to find your life more organized and true. It is vital to organize your life and to live with direction and certainty. Prioritize every aspect of your life, stick to what is truly important and delegate to others so they may be of service, too. When you spend your time on high priorities it does not become as easily filled with low priorities. Stick to the 25 percent of your activities that give you 75 percent of your desired results.

Can you think of a lesson that you have learnt the hard way about how to live a successful and happy life?

When I started out speaking over three decades ago I asked for a 'Love Donation' in exchange for my services. Boy did I learn a lesson about valuing myself. When my bowl was often left empty at the end of the evening, I realized that if I did not place a value on myself and my services, then no one else would. Instead of giving my audience the option of leaving a love donation, I starting charging a set fee. Once I valued me so did the world. The more I valued me, so did the world.

Put your heart into your work and all that you do. The most fulfilled people I've met are those who are inspired and love what they do. They act like missionaries for their work. They invest their spirit and inspiration into their interactions with all they meet, and they receive fulfilling rewards in return.

If you had your life to live over again, what would you do differently?

If I were to change any aspect of my past I would not be where I am today. I can truly say 'thank you' to my entire life. I love my life. There are no mistakes.

What significant quotes or words of wisdom most inspire you?

"Know yourself, be yourself, love yourself."

"No matter what you have done or not done you are worthy of love."

"Love what you do and do what you love."

"You deserve to live an amazing life."

Is there something we can do today to make immediate changes to our lives?

Look into your past to see if there is anything you do not feel complete with and ask yourself how that person, place, or experience has served you and how you have served others by your actions. In changing your perspective of those events, you can let go of the emotional baggage from the past and live in the present. This immediately alters the way in which you live and see the future. No matter what you have done or not done you are worthy of love. A day, a week, a month, a year, or five years later you may discover the hidden opportunities within your very challenges. But, why not have the wisdom of the ages without the aging process by looking now and discovering how everything has actually served?

Do you have a ritual that you perform on a daily basis to keep yourself positive and strong?

I have a gratitude journal, which I add to and read through every day. It is an overview of both everything I am grateful for up to that date and a vision of everything I have to look forward to in my future. It keeps me appreciative and allows me, once updated, to return to the magnificent present.

Many people would like to make a difference in the world. Where can they begin?

You make a real and meaningful difference in the world when you live your life according to your highest values and make the most of who you are as a person. When you do what you love and love what you do, you become the change you would love to see in the world. The world is already magnificent, just the way it is. There is nothing but love and all else is illusion. Love is the synthesis and synchronicity of all complementary opposites. At the end of your life you may just ask yourself a simple question, "did I do everything I could with everything I was given?" May your answer be, "Yes!"

CHAPTER 3

Happiness with effortless ease

Marci Shimoff – Happiness expert

> I believe we're all on this planet for a purpose – some people just haven't discovered theirs yet. We are here not just to survive; we are here to thrive, to live our greatest potential.

Biography

Marci Shimoff is the author of the *New York Times* bestseller, *HAPPY FOR NO REASON: 7 Steps to Being Happy from the Inside Out*, which offers a revolutionary approach to experiencing deep and lasting happiness. She is also the woman's face of the biggest self-help book phenomenon in history, *Chicken Soup for the Soul*. Her six bestselling titles in the series, including *Chicken Soup for the Woman's Soul* and *Chicken Soup for the Mother's Soul*, have met with stunning success, selling more than 14 million copies worldwide in 33 languages and have been on the *New York Times* Best Seller list for a total of 108 weeks. Marci is one of the bestselling female nonfiction authors of all time.

Marci is also a featured teacher in the international film and book phenomenon, *The Secret* and the host of the PBS television special, *Happy for No Reason*.

A celebrated transformational leader and a leading expert on happiness, success, and the law of attraction, Marci has inspired millions of people, sharing her breakthrough methods for personal fulfillment and professional success. President and co-founder of the Esteem Group, she delivers keynote addresses and seminars on self-esteem, self-empowerment, and peak performance to corporations, professional and non-profit organizations, and women's associations. She has been a top-rated trainer for numerous Fortune 500 companies, including AT&T, General Motors, Sears, Kaiser Permanente, and Bristol-Myers Squibb.

As an acclaimed authority on success and happiness, Marci is often approached by media for her insights and advice. She has been on more than 800 television and radio shows and has been interviewed for over 100 newspaper articles worldwide. Her writing has appeared in major women's magazines, including *Ladies Home Journal* and *Woman's World*.

Marci earned her MBA from UCLA and holds an advanced certificate as a stress management consultant. She is a founding member and on the board of directors of the Transformational Leadership Council, a group of 100 top leaders serving over ten million people in the self-development market.

Through her books and her presentations, Marci's message has touched the hearts and rekindled the spirits of millions of people throughout the world. She is dedicated to fulfilling her life's purpose of helping people live more empowered and joy-filled lives.

How did you start out? What early experiences shaped the person you are today?

I am fortunate, because I knew what I wanted to do with my life at a young age. When I was 13 years old, I heard a fabulous talk by a motivational speaker, Zig Ziglar. It was 1971, and I think he was the first one out there, maybe the only one at the time. As I watched him walk across that stage inspiring the audience, I knew right then that was my calling: To be a professional speaker. So I went to college and got an MBA in the field of training and development. Then I taught corporate training programs on stress management, communication skills, and leadership.

In the next stage of my career, I was blessed to meet Jack Canfield, who was an expert in the field of self-esteem, and be trained by him to teach self-esteem programs. Jack later wrote the first *Chicken Soup for the Soul* book, and when I came up with the idea for *Chicken Soup for the Women's Soul*, I got to write it with Jack and Mark Victor Hansen. It became the first specialty book in the *Chicken Soup* series, and the week it came out, it soared to #1 on the *New York Times* Best Sellers list. I went on to write five more *Chicken Soup* books and my book, *Happy for No Reason*, which together have sold over 14 million copies.

From an early age, I knew my mission was to inspire people around the world to live their highest life possible. So I knew the "what," I just didn't know the "how". I always just thought I would accomplish that as a speaker, but then through serendipity, I ended up writing books as well, and getting the opportunity to reach many more people through those books.

What do you believe to be the secret to true happiness?

The first secret to true happiness is to know that it is possible. And not only is it possible, but it is our birthright and essence. Everyone can be "Happy for No Reason," which I define as a state of peace and well-being that doesn't depend on our circumstances. This peace and well-being is our natural state, yet sadly most of us are not living it. We have gotten the idea that happiness is something you get from the outside and we have searched for it there. I believe it is our life mission, our ultimate purpose, to remove the obstructions and experience our truest essence of being Happy for No Reason. Happiness is not something you get from the outside; it is an experience you develop from within.

What is the difference between living from happiness, and living for happiness?

You could say that people who are Happy for No Reason are living from happiness. They have a peace and well-being that does not depend on their outside circumstances. This doesn't mean that they're happy all the time or have a silly grin on their face 24/7. People who are Happy for No Reason still face all the challenges of life, and they may be upset at times with sadness or grief. It's just that no matter what happens in their life, they still have that backdrop of inner peace and well-being.

On the other hand, people who are trying to get happiness *from* their life experiences are living *for* happiness. This type of happiness is transitory – it can come and go – and is not as deeply fulfilling as being able to experience the deep happiness from within. When you are happy for no reason you don't try to extract your happiness from your life experiences, rather you bring your happiness to your life experiences. You are already full on the inside and what happens on the outside is just icing on the cake.

As part of your happiness research, you have interviewed 100 remarkable people. What are some of their common characteristics?

I call the 100 people I interviewed, "the Happy 100." Looking at their lives, I found that the primary distinction between them and unhappy people is that they have different habits. I identified in them 21 core habits that anyone can practice to raise his or her happiness level. Some of the characteristics they share are a sense of lightness about them, a feeling of expansion, great vitality, openness, and a curiosity and passion for life. You feel more alive around them. They express gratitude for their blessings, even when faced with great hardship. And they are fully present, living in the "now".

What does the latest scientific research show us about happiness at a practical level?

What a beautiful question! The scientific research on happiness is wonderful these days. Science is really cracking the code of happiness.

Of all the research into happiness, I think the most exciting finding is that we each have a "happiness set point". No matter what happens on the outside, whether good or bad, your happiness level will tend to return to your happiness set-point, unless you do something consciously to change it. This set-point is determined 50 percent by your genetics, 10 percent by your circumstances, and 40 percent by your habits of thoughts and behaviors. And by changing those habits, you can raise your happiness set-point!

It's revolutionary to think that happiness can be practiced just like any other habit. In the same way you get into shape physically by changing your habits (better food choices and more trips to the gym), you can get into "happiness shape" by adopting new habits.

Most people still feel empty even though they have a fulfilling career, money or the perfect mate. Why is that?

It is because we believe in two myths: The Myth of More and The Myth of I'll be Happy When. The Myth of More leads us to think that we'll be happier when we have more of something.

And the Myth of I'll be Happy When leads us to think that we'll be happier in the future. Some examples are: I will be happy when I get a better job, I will be happy when my husband changes. I will be happy when I get a husband, I will be happy when I lose 20 pounds… and that is certainly a popular one!

According to the research, neither is true. How many people do you see with a good career, plenty of money, and the great mate, who are still unhappy? One look at Hollywood should dispel the myth that success, fame, and money are the key to happiness. These myths are based on the false belief that happiness lies outside ourselves, that it's something we have to get. It is our happiness set-point, not our circumstances that determine our happiness.

What are some happiness "robbers", and how can we avoid and/or eliminate them?

The main happiness robbers come from being stuck in old patterns of victimhood, which cause us to draw the same situation to ourselves again and again. You'll see this all the time – for example, the woman who ends up in the same type of unhealthy relationship over and over. Different man, same problems. The most common old habits that come from this victimhood are complaining, blaming, and feeling shame.

Complaining, feeling sorry for ourselves, trying to garner sympathy, or being a martyr or "over giver" are all dead giveaways that we're the guest of honor at our very own pity party. Complaining is like putting an order into the universe for more of what we don't want!

Blaming our circumstances by making excuses or blaming others for our pain or problems weakens us. We give our power away when we do this, and lose the energy we need to deal with the situation because we're directing it at someone or something else.

Feeling shame is a subtle happiness robber. When we turn blame onto ourselves, feel ashamed about things that have happened to us, or feel guilty about something we have done (or not done), we often try to suppress the pain or bury these uncomfortable feelings deep inside. This uses up a lot of energy and blocks our happiness.

You can free yourself from happiness robbers by taking these three steps:

    1.   Focus on the solution.

2. Look for the lesson and the gift in the situation.

3. Make peace with yourself.

A Japanese scientist did an experiment on the power of thought. Can you tell us about it?

The power of thought research was led by Dr. Masaru Emoto in Japan. He got water from one source and divided it into two jars. Then he had a group of people focus thoughts of appreciation and gratitude on one jar, and thoughts of hate, anger, and despair on the other jug. He then froze the water from each jar, isolated ice crystals from each, and took photographs of them using high-speed photography. The difference between the water in the two jars was dramatic. The water crystals that had been exposed to the positive thought were beautifully, symmetrically shaped. The water crystals that had been exposed to anger were very ugly, distorted and disturbing shapes. If you consider that 80 percent of our body is composed of water, you can see the importance of surrounding ourselves with positive thoughts as much as possible.

You say that we can be happy if we recognize that not all of our thoughts are true. Please explain this.

Yes, this is such an important point. We have about 60,000 thoughts a day, and for most people, 80 percent of them are negative. We have created these negative neural pathways in our brains and they become deep grooves. These old thought patterns are like tracks we've made in the snow. We keep going down the same tracks because they're there and it's easier to use them than to break new ground. But that doesn't mean they are going in the right direction. Just because we have been thinking the same thoughts for a long time, it doesn't mean that they are true. So it's important to question our conscious thoughts. Through various techniques and tools, you can question these habitual and negative patterns.

Here are some great techniques:

1. *The Work* of Byron Katie is a very simple and effective tool for questioning your thoughts and beliefs.

2. *The Sedona Method*, which is based on the premise that your thoughts and feeling aren't fact and they're not you, helps you release your limiting patterns.

3. *Emotional Freedom Technique* (EFT) is a psychotherapeutic, alternative-medicine tool based on the theory that negative emotions are caused by disturbances in the body's energy field and that tapping on the body's energy meridians while thinking of a negative emotion alters the body's energy field, restoring it to balance.

Your research shows that the happiest people are those who find and live their purpose. Why is that, and how can we do it?

I believe we're all on this planet for a purpose – some people just haven't discovered theirs yet. We are here not just to survive; we are here to thrive, to live our greatest potential. To do this, each of us needs to find our passions and follow them. There are very effective techniques you can use to do this. For example, in their book *The Passion Test,* Janet Attwood and Chris Attwood provide a simple, powerful way to clarify your passions, and live the life of your dreams.

One of my greatest mentors is my father. He was the happiest person I have ever known. He would wake up every morning with a smile on his face. He had such a passion for his career in dentistry that he didn't retire until he was 72. Many people don't live long after they retire, not just because they are older; but because they have lost their sense of purpose in life. Not my dad: he analyzed what he loved about dentistry, and realized he loved to work with his hands in artistic ways. So, at age 72, he took up needlepoint and won awards for his exquisite creations. He did needlepoint up until he died at age 91. Your passions can change over time, but living with passion at any age is a key to happiness.

How do you differentiate between a job, a career and a calling?

A job is something you do to pay the bills. It is not something you really love; it's something you do to survive. Sadly, most people are just doing a job. A career is something that uses your talent and provides some degree of fulfillment. This is better, but the ultimate kind of life's work is a calling.

A calling comes from a voice in your heart that steers you toward your mission or higher purpose. You have truly discovered why you are on this planet. While many people say they don't have a calling or don't know what their calling is, we all have a calling. Your calling will become clearer to you as you listen to your heart.

We have an inner guidance system that tells us all the time whether we are on course or off course, by sending feelings of expansion or contraction. When you feel contracted, shut down or closed, ask yourself, "Am I headed in the wrong direction?" When you feel expanded, uplifted and open, you are moving in the right direction.

How can the habit of nourishing our bodies lead to a joyful life?

Being happy is not just a state of mind – it's also a state of the body. In fact, our bodies are designed to support our happiness. The renowned neurophysiologist Dr. Candace Pert documented this mind-body-happiness link in her best-selling book, *Molecules of Emotions*. She explains that when we are happy, we are alive and literally buzzing with "happiness juices", chemicals in our body and brain that underlie our positive experiences.

There are no more powerful drugs than those you already have in your own head! More than 100,000 chemical reactions go on in your brain every second. Your brain contains a veritable pharmacopoeia of natural happiness-enhancing drugs: Endorphins are the brain's painkiller, three times more powerful than morphine! Serotonin naturally calms anxiety and relieves depression, and dopamine promotes alertness and a feeling of enjoyment. And there are many others as well. They are just waiting for the right conditions in order to be released to every organ and cell in your body. Because your brain's pharmacy is open twenty-four hours a day, you can create your own supply of these happiness chemicals anytime you want.

Studies abound showing how everyday activities – singing, listening to relaxing music, stroking a pet, getting a massage, enjoying a long hug, gardening – increase our happiness chemicals. Even smiling raises our happiness levels!

You have said that being happy is good for our health. In what way is that true?

Let me share with you some very interesting statistics about happiness and health:

Happy people are 35 percent less likely to get a cold, and they produce 50 percent more antibodies in response to flu vaccines than the average person.

Individuals who score high on happiness and optimism scales have a reduced risk of cardiovascular disease, hypertension, and infections.

People who maintain a sense of humor, an indication of inner happiness, outlive those who don't, and the survival edge is particularly large for people with cancer.

One study showed that a sense of humor cut a cancer's patient's chance of premature death by about 70 percent.

These are just a few examples of the many ways happiness improves our health and increases our longevity.

Why is it difficult for most people to be happy in their daily lives?

We've just got some bad habits that create stress and reduce our energy. Just take a look at our lives. Most of us zip around like over-caffeinated bees, multitasking madly and grabbing meals on the run. Our stressful lifestyles, which include unhealthy eating and a lack of exercise and proper rest, hinder our ability to create happy cells.

Stress is a huge happiness robber and drain on our health. Scientific evidence indicates that 90 percent of all diseases are stress related. So many of us are stressed out and exhausted, yet we ignore our symptoms and power on through the day, taking medication to dull the pain without dealing with the deeper issue.

Then there are the environmental toxins we're exposed to every day: chemicals in our processed food, pesticides in our produce, hormones and antibiotics in our meat and milk, and polluted air and water. Many of these foreign elements accumulate in our system and have an adverse effect on our health. We need to have habits that will counteract the stress and create happiness in our cells.

What is the best advice you have ever received?

I once asked my father, "Dad, what is the best advice you can give me for life?"

He turned to me and said four words: "Honey, just be happy".

I looked at him and said, "That's easy for you to say. You were just born that way, but I wasn't. What should I do?"

He said four more words, "Honey, I don't know."

While he didn't know how I could experience greater happiness, he certainly knew that it was the priority in life. I spent the last 30 years finding out the answer to that question: How could I be happier, how could anyone be happier? In the process, my own happiness level has increased tremendously. If you make it a priority, yours will too. At the end of your life, this is what you will ask yourself: Did I live a happy life? That will be what will matter.

Who is Dr Viktor Frankl, and how did his life inspire and help you?

I was first introduced to Victor Frankl's life-changing ideas in high school when my English teacher had our class read his book, *Man's Search for Meaning*. Frankl was a Holocaust survivor who wrote with incredible eloquence about how he and others rose above despair while enduring the daily atrocities of life in a Nazi concentration camp. At first, I resisted reading the book, afraid I would be too horrified by his account, but with each page I felt my heart lift as I became more and more inspired. His great turning point came when he realized that the one thing no one could take away from him was his choice to remain loving in the face of whatever was done to him and those around him.

If Viktor Frankl could find meaning – and even experience genuine love – in the worst circumstances imaginable, then I have to believe that we can all find courage each day to change how we respond to whatever happens in our lives. His name says it all. He was the ultimate Victor!

Is there a significant quote of saying that you live your life by?

There are two quotes I especially love, one by Sri Ramakrishna: "The winds of grace are always blowing, but you have to raise the sail." And a beautiful one from Albert Einstein: "There are only two ways to live your life. One is as though nothing is a miracle. The other is as though everything is a miracle."

Do you have a ritual that you perform on a daily basis to keep yourself positive and strong?

I do many rituals. I believe that my habits or daily rituals keep me living a life of joy and fulfillment. Some of my daily rituals are waking up with gratitude, exercising, meditating, eating healthy food, and drinking plenty of water. When I go to sleep early, it makes a huge difference in the way I feel the next day. When possible I breathe fresh air, I breathe in nature. I sing, I move my body, I do work that is my calling, I look for the lessons or gifts in every situation. And what's incredibly important is that I surround myself with other happy people

Why is it important to cultivate feelings of gratitude?

Making a habit of feeling gratitude is the fast track to happiness. What you appreciate, appreciates. According to the law of attraction what you put your attention on will grow stronger in your life. What you are grateful for is what you will attract to you. So, the quickest way to be happier is to focus on all that you have to be grateful for.

Who is your greatest teacher and/or hero and why?

That would be my father, a truly loving and good human being. He is my #1 Happy for No Reason role model.

What is your vision of an ideal world?

I envision a world in where every person feels the love, joy, and happiness in their own hearts and souls. A world in which all people are living in a state of peace. We can each make a difference in this world by being happy ourselves, as this Chinese proverb expresses:

> If there is light in the soul,
>
> there will be beauty in the person.
>
> If there is beauty in the person,
>
> there will be harmony in the house.

If there is harmony in the house,

there will be order in the nation.

If there is order in the nation,

there will be peace in the world.

Many people would like to make a difference in the world. Where can they begin?

In the beautiful, immortal words of Mahatma Gandhi, "Be the change you want to see in the world." Where to begin? Take your first baby steps in that direction today – not tomorrow, take them today. We start by enlightening ourselves first; that is how we change the world. Once you start practicing the habits of happiness, you will find your happiness level rising. You will see in a very short time how much happier you and the people around you are. You will be the light that shows the way for others too.

The truly happy people I know contribute something greater than themselves in life. When Stewart Emery interviewed people with enduring success and happiness for his book, *Success Built to Last*, he found that their goals weren't fame, wealth, or power. People with those goals sometimes ended up living empty and unhappy lives. Truly happy people live fully and passionately, engaged in meaningful service to a larger cause. Oprah Winfrey once said, "I never went for the money, I just said, 'God use me. Show me how to take who I am, who I want to be, and what I can do, and use it for a greater purpose, greater than myself.'"

Happiness is our essence. My wish for everyone is that they experience a life that is Happy for No Reason, with the kind of lasting joy that Shirley Cesar speaks of in this quote: "This joy that I have, the world didn't give it to me, and the world can't take it away."

CHAPTER 4

Science with a spiritual twist

Fred Alan Wolf – Quantum Physicist

> I see life as a kind of gigantic wave that we either learn to surf upon or get pushed along by.

Biography

Fred Alan Wolf, PhD is as a physicist, writer, and lecturer whose work in quantum physics and consciousness has become well known through his popular and scientific writing. Dr. Wolf is widely regarded for his simplification of the new physics. His book *Taking the Quantum Leap* was the recipient of the prestigious National Book Award for Science. Dr. Wolf's fascination with the world of physics began one afternoon when, as a child at a local matinee, the newsreel revealed the awesome power and might of the world's first atomic explosion. This fascination continued, leading Wolf to study mathematics and physics. He is the author of sixteen books and audio CDs including his latest works: *The Yoga of Time Travel, Dr. Quantum's Little Book of Big Ideas,* the audio CD series: *Dr. Quantum Presents: Do-it-Yourself Time Travel, Dr. Quantum Presents: A User's Guide to Your Universe,* and *Dr. Quantum Presents: Meet the Real Creator: You.*

A former professor of physics at San Diego State University, Dr. Wolf now lectures, teaches, and conducts research worldwide. He was featured as the resident physicist on The Discovery Channel's *The Know Zone* and is a regular guest on many radio talkshows and television shows across the USA and abroad. He has also appeared on the nationally syndicated PBS series *Closer to Truth*. He appeared in the 2003 Special Collectors Edition of the Paramount Studio DVD movie *Star Trek IV on Disc 2 Time Travel: The Art of the Possible*. He also appears in the full length feature film starring Oscar winner Marlee Matlin, *What The Bleep Do We Know!?* produced by Lord of the Wind Productions. He can also be seen in the feature films *The Secret* and *Down the Rabbit Hole* as well as in several other films.

In academia, Dr. Wolf has challenged minds at San Diego State University, the University of Paris, the Hebrew University of Jerusalem, the University of London's Birkbeck College, and many other institutions of higher learning. Wolf is best known for his contributions in technical papers and popular books, but he is frequently in demand as a lecturer, keynote speaker, and consultant to industry and the media.

How did you start our? What early experiences shaped the person you are today?

As a child I was interested in magic–the kind performed by great stage magicians. I suffered from stammering and I would practice magic in front of a mirror to overcome my speech impediment. I also practiced breathing exercises and meditation taught to me by a gifted speech teacher – although the meditation technique wasn't called that when I was a child.

From these two interests I developed a fascination with the great magic show known as physics. The "trick" that most captured my attention was the first atomic bomb explosion in New Mexico that I saw in a newsreel in Chicago – my home town – when I was 10 years old. I wanted to know how to do this "trick" and as I began to understand it, I learned it was called atomic physics. I wanted to know more "tricks" so I studied physics as an undergraduate and then as a graduate student going on to receive my PhD degree. My overwhelming desire was to not only study the great mysteries of physics – especially quantum physics – but to be able to perform these "tricks" in front of an audience.

My life has been a continuing journey of realization of those desires through writing books, giving visual and audio presentations in lectures, movies, books, audio courses, and TV. In brief, I am doing what I want to do and that brings me great joy.

What do you believe is the best way for a person to find their purpose in life?

I think we discover our purpose by finding the course of action that brings us great joy while simultaneously providing a service to others. This takes faith and perseverance and many simply do not wish to put in the effort. Often a stumbling block will crop up as we take our journey through life. For some of us, this obstacle is a great gift that when overcome enables us to realize our desires. Others may become completely discouraged and give up. In failing to recognize the opportunity that such a stumbling block provides, many settle for second best, or worse, and give up on their dreams.

What do you believe to be the true secret of happiness?

Learning to fulfill your desires is the real secret. Having the patience to learn the skills necessary to fulfill those desires establishes you firmly on the road to happiness. I am personally happiest when I am learning things, especially if they are not easy things to master. While engaged in the process of discovery I am truly happy. If you have learned something so well that things no longer capture your interest, you can easily become unhappy. If you feel you have nothing more to learn in your life, and you are unhappy as a result of this, then the key is to learn how to use your talents to assist others in learning your skill.

How do you define genuine success?

Paradoxically, achieving success isn't all you might wish it to be. The one thing that keeps me most happy is not achieving success - it is the road I travel and not the destination that is most important in this sense. Most people I know who one would call successful are - for the most part - constant failures. The major difference is they know how to fail and in fact look forward to failure as something new to learn so they can continue on the path to achievement. It is very hard, for example, for Nobel prize winners to keep up their sense of happiness, since once having won the honour they begin thinking of themselves as second best or as "has-beens". Having already made a billion dollars or achieved some other lofty goal, most people find themselves somewhat aimless for a wile, wondering what they should do next.

What is quantum physics, in a nutshell?

It's the physics that all fundamental matter and energetic interactions must follow. It surprised everyone who had anything to do with quantum physics to discover that fundamental matter did not follow strict cause and effect rules when any interactions took place; what happened before didn't necessarily produce what happened next or what might occur in the future.

The truly surprising fact of quantum physics is that the living observer disturbs the material universe, and all observable interactions in it, by the mere act of observing. These acts are called the *observer effect*. Since mind is needed in order for observation to occur, mind and matter are not independent of each other. Each of us creates our own realities simply because our realities depend on how our minds and brains "see" and interpret the world around us. Most important here is not the action of observation of large, massive bodies, but the action of observation involved in the brain when we observe our own behavior and the behavior of others.

How can quantum physics help us to live a more happy and peaceful life?

The fact that observers of the material universe can alter it by their acts of observation means that by using your powers of observation you can change situations that make you unhappy by looking at them in a different light. While the observer effect strictly applies in the quantum physics realm of refined atomic and subatomic interactions, it may just as well apply in the arena of human interactions. The way we respond – in body and mind – to our environment is influenced by how we think and feel in any given situation.

This observer effect then may be most applicable to the manner in which you choose to think about yourself and others. By thinking about yourself or others in a negative way, you will begin to modify and observe your behavior to match the way you think. Hence by changing your thinking you can change your behavior – in essence become a happier person who is at peace with your neighbors no matter how close or far they are from you. Peace, then, is just a natural result of being happier with your self.

You compare the events of life to gigantic waves in the ocean. How does understanding the rules of quantum physics help us live better?

Conscious life appears as excitations of waves in a great ocean of consciousness. The great sea of consciousness is called the quantum field of mind. Like an invisible ocean, it permeates everything, so rather than saying we are containers of consciousness, with this consciousness located as individual minds within separate bodies, it is more accurate to say that the sea of consciousness contains us. This gives us the ever-present feeling or basic "hum" of realization that none of us is truly separate from any other. It also provides us with faith that we – the great consciousness – carry on even after the death of the bodies that carry that "sea". I call this learning to surf the ocean of the great mind rather than being swept over by it as victims.

What can the latest scientific research tell us about how to live happier lives, at a practical level?

The question really is: What do you think you are? Who do you think you are? And can you change who the observer is that you think you are? The whole idea behind quantum physics is that the observer affects that which is being observed. Therefore, if you can change how you go about observing what you call your life, you can change the reality that you're living in.

Here is a simple example. Let's say that right now you're sitting and you're thinking to yourself, "I'm so depressed. I feel so bad. I feel terrible." To change this experience, you can just do one simple thing. Simply ask yourself this question: "*Who* is feeling depressed?" You don't need to answer the question. Just posing it without answering changes the chemistry inside your body. Just by asking, you can begin to lift yourself out of that depression. However, you've got to keep doing it for a while because it isn't like an automatic pilot. You can't throw a switch one time and expect the happiness current to continuously flow. You've got to keep doing it, and after a while you begin to realize that the person who is saying "I am depressed" is not you.

Based on your understanding, what is the nature of reality?

In its most essential state, reality is nonmaterial, and yet it has the ability to project matter and separate minds into existence. Both are projections from this deeper reality. The reality we perceive seems to be a projection from something deeper and thus more mysterious. The essential mystery of it lies in two axioms of our thinking. They are: 1) Why is there *something* rather than *nothing*? 2) There is spirit in all things, and all things are at the same time within that spirit. The spirit that underlies all material things is becoming more apparent to physicists as we gain an increased understanding of the quantum fields of mind and matter.

The idea is that all human experiences are projections from a single mind. In spite of our perceived differences, we are the same "person", only we appear at seemingly different places and different times. These appearances are not a true picture of the situation but only a projection of the deeper truth that only a few of us perceive at very rare moments, if at all.

What is consciousness?

No one can say what consciousness is; in fact, no one can say what anything is. The verb *is* pertains to equivalence or to the simple equal sign ($=$) in mathematics. I can say x is 5 or $x=5$ and most of us would know what I mean. However, when I say, "I am Fred Alan Wolf," I surely do not mean that is all I am. After all, "Fred Alan Wolf" is merely a name with no more meaning than the breaths of air and vocal-chord vibrations used to speak those three words. From day to day, hour to hour, second to second, who and what I am changes. I am surely more than a name, or a profession, or someone's designated spouse. In quantum physics, we also cannot say what an electron or a molecule or any fundamental particle *is*. We can only say what these particles *do* – that is, how they behave in certain circumstances. Beyond that, no one really knows what these things *are*.

Today we believe that all fundamental particles are excitations in a potential existence called the quantum field, which fills the universe. Each particle has its own field. For example, there are quark fields, electron fields, and photon fields. We have this picture simply because we are able to make observations of matter that support these pictures. At best, these pictures are metaphors that provide simple word-images of what we observe.

How different is the world of quantum physics from the physical world we see?

Think of it this way: Your computer works at your command, causing images to magically appear on your screen when you press a button or a key. However, what you see on the screen is not what is really happening in the microprocessors of the computer. This is precisely the relationship between quantum physics and the world we see. Just as we will ourselves to move or think or feel or sense the world around us, inside of us a world of psychophysical processes goes on, despite the fact that we are hardly aware of its existence. The world of quantum physics is a world of seeming paradoxes and mysteries that our ordinary minds are normally not capable of understanding. Even physicists have trouble understanding quantum physics because its axioms run counter to our normal reasoning.

Could you please explain the concept of "mind into matter"?

The basic idea is that matter itself cannot exist without a mind to perceive it. Without mind, matter would not appear as the solid hunks of stuff that we perceive in our everyday world. Instead, matter would remain in the state of potential reality but never as actual particles. Hence mind must enter into matter in order to be perceived by us.

How does creation occur at quantum level?

It turns out that the vacuum of empty space is quite unstable. Accordingly it erupts, producing particles and antiparticles in a very rapid succession which quickly recombine back into nothing. This occurs especially at the tiniest volumes of space and smallest intervals of time as, for example, in the nucleons of every atom. These eruptions of matter and antimatter provide the necessary forces that hold the nucleons together and make up a field of force called the gluon field. Without this field no actual nucleons would form and without nucleons no atoms would form and that would mean complete and total chaos and no universe.

Do you agree that our thoughts create our reality?

Not quite. The question is: what do we mean by "create"? In quantum physics, we know that matter itself arises from quantum fields – that these field "create" the particles we call matter as if they were excitations of this field. If we accept that this quantum field is a field of consciousness, then we could say that matter arises out of mind. However, if we say that the mind creates thoughts in the same way, we might make the mistake of saying that thoughts create matter, which is not the case. If by "create" we mean that we have a thought and then some appropriate action arises due to this thought, we might again say that thought creates the reality of our actions. It would be more correct to say that thought, action, and matter arise from a field of consciousness than to say that thought creates reality.

From your view, what is the best and most practical method of manifesting our goals?

Practice hitting your mark and developing good gamesmanship by learning how to play your game better. Usually this means learning how to make the most of your natural skills. If you watch a good athlete carefully you will see that most of the skill in the athlete's performance comes from practice, practice, practice – in the training room, as part of the athlete's daily routine. Achieving goals occurs in much the same way, by refining our skills, just as an athlete would do. When I am writing books, I spend several hours every day working and typing and thinking and putting words down. I also spend several hours going over what I wrote and rewriting. Have faith in this practice. It will never let you down.

How do the conscious and subconscious minds shape the events in our lives?

In the same way the universe creates matter and antimatter, ideas, thoughts, and feelings arise within our unconscious minds. However, our willful, conscious minds dictate whether we will or will not give credence to what our unconscious minds dream up. In this manner, Nature is both creative and destructive. It tends to balance out positive and negative thoughts and feelings just as it balances out matter and antimatter. Because we have free will, we have the power to pay more attention to one and less to the other. Hence we have both dreamers and skeptics. Both exist within you, and you have surely practiced paying more attention to one rather than the other. This practice has shaped your perception and the point of view you hold toward life and the world.

Do you believe that events in life happen randomly or are predestined?

Both are true. I see life as a kind of gigantic wave that we either learn to surf upon or get pushed along by. To the extent that you learn how the wave operates you can become a better surfer and even control the direction the wave takes you. If you fight the wave or lose sight that it exists, you find yourself feeling hopeless or powerless and you may get the feeling that life is a random mess. If you learn to surf masterly, you can get the illusion that you are controlling it and thereby assume you are a great master or business person or some other fantasy. Both of these are illusions.

What is intuition?

I define intuition as the ability to intuit the possible future and make choices as a result of what we perceive may happen next. We all have intuition—without this "sense", none of us would be here. After millions of years of evolution it follows logically that perceiving into the near future imparts a distinct survival advantage to those who have this ability. Neurophysiology also indicates to us that we have the ability to sense the immediate future. Consciousness itself may not exist as a point-like ability to perceive single events at specific times and places, but there is a field of consciousness that perceives over a window of time and space rather than as single pixel of information.

Is it true that the very act of observing events in your life can alter their outcome?

Yes it is true but it doesn't work the way you may think. In a popular con game called 3-card Monte, the con man will be behind a little table upon which he throws three playing cards all face down. One of the cards is red-faced – say the queen of hearts. The other two are black – say the ace of clubs and ace of spades. He asks you to bet your money on picking out the queen. He shows you the cards and then he throws them face down and mixes them up on the table. Because he has a tricky way of throwing the cards it is not obvious which card is the queen. If you watch the game you may think that perhaps you can detect the card… but what if you are wrong? Both thoughts arise in your mind, just as antimatter and matter pop up in the vacuum. You may just resign yourself to not making a bet. But then another person comes up and starts betting and winning more times than he loses. You then watch and sure enough, you find yourself more often than not making all the right choices. Now you decide to put your money on the table. The mere fact that another person was observing and playing in the game changed the way you thought about it, and as a result, you took a new action. The problem, of course, is that the other person was in on the con and the two were out to get you to place a bet. Once you went all in, the con man who was throwing the cards would use a tricky move to fool you.

The point is that observers tend to see what others are already observing and take action based on what others are doing. Hence the ups and downs of the stock market – including the economic recession of 2008–09 – are based on the level of our perceived confidence. If Joe won't buy then why should I? If Joe won't start a new business then why should I?

Please describe your thoughts on the law of attraction? Does like attract like?

No, that is not correct from a physical point of view. "Like attracts like" only reflects one aspect of the way the spiritual and physical universe works. Not only do we need a law of attraction but we also need a law of repulsion, otherwise everything would collapse to one big lump. In certain stars where gravity overcomes electromagnetic repulsion, such collapses do occur and they form black holes or neutron stars. None of us want to live in one.

In quantum physics we find that like doesn't attract like. For example, like electrical charges and like magnetic poles repel each other (+ repels + and – repels –) and unlike charges and poles attract (+ attracts –). Indeed, if things didn't repel each other at some short distance, there wouldn't be a universe of separate things. Even the proton and neutron (which attract to make the strong nuclear force) repel each other if they get too close. Hence if you use the metaphor without thinking you may find that being a saint (+), you will attract a lot of sinners (–s).

However, there is a rather strange exception in quantum physics that affects both attraction and repulsion, which doesn't have anything to do with charges or electricity or magnetism. Here we find like things attracting each other and other like things repelling each other. It turns out that particles of light called photons attract each other while particles of matter called electrons repel each other in a certain way of thinking. Photons "like" to be in the same quantum physical state, while electrons "hate" to be in the same quantum physical state. Without both of these properties, atoms could not form, our universe would not work, and life as we know it would be impossible. Particles that attract each other in this strange manner are called bosons and particles that repel each other are called fermions.

How can we begin to live an inspiring life?

By "breathing" well and fully; by taking into our systems as much as we can and thereby learning more about ourselves and our abilities, as well as learning about the worlds which lie outside our immediate environments. I find inspiration by doing this every day. To me, a day lived without learning something new or renewing something forgotten is a day wasted; too many of these days will leave you uninspired and gasping for spiritual air. Inspiration also requires that we learn to expire – to let go of the waste products that only pollute our lives. These include thoughts or feelings that lead us to believe we are less than anything we care to compare ourselves with.

Is there a significant quote or saying that you live your life by?

"Row, row, row your boat, gently down the stream; merrily, merrily, merrily, merrily, life is but a dream."

Do you have a ritual that you perform on a daily basis to keep yourself positive and strong?

I do, and it is very simple. I live in the highest state of consciousness possible. To understand how I attain this state, let me first label the three states of consciousness (most humans operate within the first state): (I) Ordinary consciousness—you want an apple and thus you have to work to earn money to get an apple; (II) Higher consciousness—you want an apple, and somebody comes to you and gives you an apple; and (III) Highest state of consciousness—you want an apple and it appears instantly.

Has anyone ever gotten to (III)? I know I have gotten to (II) because there have been times when I have wanted a thing, and someone has brought me that very thing. However, I don't really know if that was due to my really wanting the thing or if I just saw into the future that someone would bring it to me. Or, possibly what happened was this: when I received the thing, that action created in my mind the realization that I had unconsciously wanted it.

The trick to attaining (II) is to want what you already have and leave the rest to your unknowable consciousness to fulfill the desire for what you don't have. Then, whenever (II) happens, it is a delight.

Now let's consider (III), the highest state of consciousness possible. Everything in my life has to do with whatever I desire to do (II) and what I work for when I apply appropriate action when in state (I). Since I desire this state of putting effort toward my goals (II) and taking action on the things (I) that I value in life, I therefore manifest what I want every day (III=I+II). Thus, I have reached the highest state of consciousness (III), because what I want is instantly appearing in my life. It works so well that I don't even have to want it or long for it or wish it to be so. It just is. I am in the business of "Isness".

CHAPTER 5

Overcoming adversity and winning the business of life

Bill Bartmann – Billionaire Business Coach

> *Self belief is the strongest, most powerful force in the world.*

Biography

Bill Bartmann is the ultimate underdog/survivor/achiever, overcoming personal circumstances and tragedy to rise to the top enterprise in America. Homeless at age 14, a member of a street gang and a high-school dropout, Bill took control of his life by taking the GED exam and putting himself through college and law school. Bill is the "Billionaire Business Coach". He is the only self-made billionaire who has exclusively devoted his life to teaching others. Bill is the leading authority on entrepreneurship in America. He has created seven successful businesses in seven different industries; these include a $3.5 billion, 3,900 employee international company that he started from his kitchen table with a $13,000 loan.

He has been named National Entrepreneur of the Year by NASDAQ, *USA Today*, Merrill Lynch, and the Kauffman Foundation. His companies have been named by *Inc. Magazine* as one of the 500 Fastest Growing Companies in America – four years in a row. He has been awarded a permanent place in the Smithsonian Institute's Museum of American History and awarded the American Academy of Achievement's Golden Plate Award as one of the Outstanding Achievers of the 21st Century.

He now travels the country, sharing his story of how he created his success and how he dealt with his challenges. Bill has been credited with single handedly changing and reforming the collection industry in America. His new mission, just as ambitious, is to "reverse the business failure rate in America".

Millions of people have seen Bill on ABC, NBC, CBS, FOX News, CNN, and CNBC. Bill's expertise has been featured on TV with Shepard Smith, Neil Cavuto, and Donny Deutsch. He has been profiled in *Forbes, Fortune, Inc., Bloomberg BusinessWeek, The New Yorker, People, Wall Street Journal, US News & World Report*, and *USA Today*.

How did you start out? What early experiences shaped the person you are today?

To say that I came from a humble beginning would be an understatement. I was one of eight children. My father was a janitor and my mother cleaned other people's homes, just to help provide for the necessities, and we still didn't have enough money to live on. Once a month I would go with my father to stand in line at the government's "Foodstuffs Commodity Program" distribution center, where we waited for our allotment of dried beans, canned meat, powdered milk, and processed cheese. My family moved into eight different rental houses during the first fourteen years of my life, and several of those moves were required because the city condemned the house we were living in at the time as being unfit for human habitation.

I left home when I was fourteen and joined a traveling carnival. During my teen years I began smoking and drinking, and I became a member of a gang. I spent five and a half years in high school and never graduated. I had a hearing defect that went undiagnosed until I tried to join the military at age seventeen. That same year, I fell down a flight of stairs in a drunken stupor and ended up in the hospital, paralyzed.

Ultimately, my life changed for the better. I eventually received my GED, put myself through college, and made it through law school. I practiced law for five years and decided to move my career in another direction. At the request of a bank, I took over a foreclosed oilfield pipe manufacturing plant in Oklahoma and turned it into a million-dollar-a-month business – that is, until OPEC slashed the price of oil, which left me out of business and a million dollars in debt. I ended up filing for bankruptcy.

That was when I saw financial opportunities in another business sector that was failing – savings and loans that were being bought out by the federal government. My wife Kathy and I began buying bad debt from these failed financial institutions and collecting on the debts from our kitchen table. We found success almost immediately and grew the company very quickly. By the late 1990s, we had 3,900 employees, and the company had revenues in excess of $1 billion and earnings of over $182 million.

In the present economic climate, this same opportunity has presented itself again, and this time I'm teaching others how to buy and collect bad debt. My mission is to "reverse the business failure rate in America".

What do you believe is the best way for a person to find their purpose in life?

In order to find your purpose in life you have to ask yourself a few questions and be willing to answer them honestly. What is it you really want to do? If you are not consciously aware of what you want to do in life, then you can't discover your purpose. Many people say, "If money was no object, what would you like to be doing?" The answer to this question is usually found in whatever it is that gets you fired up, that charges your motor and causes you to say, "I'd do this even if they didn't pay me to do it."

Beyond asking yourself what kind of work you want to do, you also need to determine what kind of lifestyle you want to have; furthermore, what's your definition of success? You have to ask yourself these questions in order to really understand yourself. The answers to these questions will help you discover the things you are most passionate about. Out of your passions will come your purpose. Do something that you can be passionate about and you will be successful.

Remember, don't limit yourself. Having high self-esteem is very important to fulfilling your dreams and accomplishing your goals. Don't worry about *how* you're going to fulfill your purpose; just believe that you can, and as you pursue your passions, the *how* will fall into place.

What do you believe is the most powerful force in the world?

Self-belief is the strongest, most powerful force in the world. From this power, all other things flow. Every invention, creation, and thing of utility known to humanity was spawned by a belief in the mind of the people who accepted the concept that they could actually create or cause things to happen. If they did not have this belief, they would not have the ability to withstand the frustrations that are always a part of this process. Without belief, they would have succumbed to the jeers and doubts of others as they progressed on the road to completion.

Self-belief (or self-esteem) is the internal image our subconscious mind has of itself, as it relates to how we feel about our personal capabilities to accomplish certain tasks. This image can be both positive and negative. If you could see what I see when I look at you, you would see a person who is smart, strong, dedicated, loyal, caring, and most importantly, capable of accomplishing any goal you set for yourself. I see a person with the power and talents to do anything you set your mind to. This power is within you and always has been within you. You doubt you have this power because you don't recognize it. Believe it or not, this is perfectly normal. Ninety-nine percent of the people in the world doubt their own abilities. That is why almost every major accomplishment in history had been made by the other 1 percent.

Who are some of the people in history that understand the power of self-belief?

Here is a list of people who understood the power of self-belief:

Alexander the Great believed he could conquer the world.

Christopher Columbus believed he could find a new passage to India.

Wilbur and Orville Wright believed they could fly.

Abraham Lincoln believed he could be president of the USA.

Henry Ford believed he could create the largest company in the world.

Ray Kroc believed he could sell billions of hamburgers.

Billy Graham believed he could create a global ministry.

Bill Gates believed he could become the richest man in the world.

    This list of achievers was chosen because these people were not taller, smarter, better looking, younger, or in any aspects different than you and the rest of the people on earth. That one respect was their total, unrestricted belief in themselves. They did not think that they "might" succeed or "maybe" they would succeed or "if" something happened then they would succeed; they absolutely believed they were going to succeed. This belief is so strong that they conducted their daily life as if success were a certainty. For them it was only a matter of time. Even when they didn't know how, they still always knew they would. Their self-belief was so strong that no amount of adversity or frustration could stop these people from continuing their quest. No setback, how matter how devastating, stopped these people from believing that they would accomplish their goals.

How can our self-belief influence the outcome of our lives?

Let me give you an example of how our self-belief can influence the outcome. When I was a freshman in high school, I wrestled at the ninety-eight-pound level. As part of the wrestling practice workout, the coach wanted all of us to do weight-lifting exercises. Each session involved doing a number of standard lifts, including one called bench press. In this exercise, you lay your back on a bench, lower the weight-lifting bar to your chest, and then push the weight upward by extending your arms. I had done this exercise with 125 pounds of weight during the wrestling season. Each time I tried to go the level of 130 pounds; I would fail and be unable to perform the exercise. Every time I tried a heavier weight, I was unable to lift.

One day as I was finishing my warm up workout at a lower level, one of my wrestling buddies walked by as I was lying flat on the bench, and I asked him to put on some extra weights. I had been warming up with 100 pounds of weight on the bar. I asked him to add an extra 25 pounds. While I was catching my breath and not paying attention, he deliberately put on fifty pounds instead of twenty five pounds. When he told me that the weights were properly on, I began my lift. I performed it smoothly and flawlessly even though it was 25 pounds heavier than I had ever previously lifted!

Where did the extra strength come from? It was there all the time. My mind had become conditioned to my weight limitation and was impeding me from lifting anything heavier. Once my mind was deceived – thinking there were only 125 pounds on the bar, when in fact there were 150 – it allowed me to lift it.

How would you define the mind?

A pure definition of "mind" is difficult to formulate, as this term has been used by many different ways throughout history. The different ways of referring to the mind began the same time as when humans became aware we had a mind. Terms like brain, mind, intellect, and soul have often been used interchangeably. The debate over this definition has raged over centuries, from philosophers such as Aristotle, Plato, and Thomas Moore, to psychiatrists and psychologists such as Freud to Jung. Even today, neurosurgeons debate with philosophers and theologians as to the most correct definition.

It is not my intent to find an answer to this centuries-old problem but rather to explain how this amazing function of the mind is accomplished, regardless of the current definition. For our purposes, we will refer to the brain as that biological mass of cells and nerves located within our cranium. We will refer to the mind as the thing (or process) that allows us memories and creates thought. While the mind may be located within the brain itself, it is not the brain. It is instead a process involving chemical and electrical responses affecting various parts of the brain, which then allow us to initiate and control our physical functions.

What do you think is one of them most overlooked secrets of success?

One of the simplest, and yet most important, secrets of achieving an objective is to keep it in sight. We have all heard the expression "keep your eye on the prize" or "stay focused". Of all the secret of success, this one is the most overlooked, most under appreciated, and most misunderstood. By staying focused through reinforcing our desire to achieve, accomplish or obtain this prize that has become the object of our promise, we enlist our mind to help us become the object of our promise.

The mind is a marvelous and powerful device. We have discovered that the human brain has over a hundred billion nerve cells. The total number of synapses in the cortex of one person is 10_{th} to 15_{th} power (10,000,000,000,000,000), or about 200,000 times the population of us humans on earth. Although we don't fully understand how it does what it does, we do know that the human mind is more complicated than any supercomputer ever devised and is faster and more efficient than any as well.

How can we use the mind for creative and practical purposes?

We have learned from our prior life experiences that if we concentrate on something – stay focused on something and continue to think about something – eventually we begin to find a solution. This solution didn't come to us by voodoo or magic, but rather, as we focused on a particular desired result, we sent continuous repeat messages to our mind that we are looking for a particular solution. Eventually, the mind shows us the solution we are seeking.

Mental vision is the ability of the human mind to display and record an event in a person's mind as if this event has actually occurred, when in fact it has not yet occurred. The sound, color, and acting in this production rival anything yet produced by Hollywood.

We can use our mental vision to feel the results of accomplishing an objective before it has actually been achieved. As we engaged in mental vision, we are bombarding your senses with the feeling of success. This internally generated data becomes real to the memory bank of the mind and will be filed as an event that really occurred. As such, it will be one of the pieces of information that the mind will recall when it inquires as to whether we are capable of accomplishing our objectives.

You mentioned that many great sportsmen and businessmen use mental vision as a part of their daily routine. Can you give us an example?

Tiger Woods uses this technique before every golf shot. In the book, *Think Like Tiger* by John Andrisani, Tiger explains how he engages in mental vision prior to each and every shot. During his practice swing, Tiger mentally watches the club's head hit the ball and the ball leave the club's head. His mental vision doesn't end there; he continues to visualize not only the trajectory of the ball while in flight but also how it will roll once it lands on the ground. Only after he has seen this complete picture will he perform the actual shot. How can your mind help you accomplish what you want unless it knows what it looks like? Once your subconscious mind can "see" what it is you want, it will figure out what it needs to do to help you achieve it.

Why is self-honesty one of the most important lessons we have to learn in life?

I think the most important of all is to be honest with yourself. Make sure the thing you are about to say you want to accomplish is really what you want to accomplish. Don't set your objective to please someone else – set it to please you. Yes, it is nice to make others happy, and it is nice to do nice things for others. But when you are talking about your life's objective, the first person you need to be able to satisfy is yourself. As Shakespeare said: "To thine own self be true, and thou canst not then be false to any man." So many people go through life trying to make others happy and never end up achieving their own happiness. Your life and your existence is all you are and all you have – why give it away? Instead, achieve your objective – your life's promise – and then spend time, effort, money, or whatever is necessary to help those to whom you feel so obligated. Give them the things you reap from your success – don't give them your life.

We all know boys in little league who are there not because they want to be, but instead, they are there to make their dads happy. We all know little girls who take ballet lessons because they want to make their mothers happy. We know sons and daughters of businessmen, lawyers, and doctors who majored in business, law, and medicine in college and then pursued a business career, a legal career, or a medical career – to please one or both of their parents, even though they would have preferred doing something else with their lives. We all know women who work forty-plus hours a week who would rather be home raising their children.

We only have one life to live. Why spend most of it pursuing something only to accomplish it and then find out we really didn't want it, or we really could have done something different? What a shame, and what a waste of the most valuable of all of your resources – your very existence!

Please share with us some advice for setting and achieving goals.

Once you decide what you want to do or become or achieve, you must define your promise, your objective – the thing you want to accomplish – with a high degree of clarity and specificity. The more specifically defined the target is, the easier it will be to achieve. You cannot hit a target unless you can clearly identify it. The childhood game of pin the tail on the donkey demonstrates how difficult it is to try to hit a target you can't see. Once the blindfold has been removed and the target is clearly visible, pinning the tail in the right location is remarkably simple. Trying to achieve an objective that is poorly defined is like an archer trying to hit the bull's-eye of a target he can't see.

Imagine yourself standing at the twenty-yard line of a football stadium with a bow and a quiver full of arrows in your hand. Twenty yards away in the end zone is an archery target. As you shoot your first arrow, you will note whether you are shooting too high, too low, too much to the right, or too much to the left. Your second arrow will then be adjusted accordingly to correct the previous error. Your third arrow will be adjusted even more precisely. After each shot, you will take what you have learned from the previous shots and make your future adjustments accordingly. With this constant adjustment for error, you will eventually be able to hit the target.

Now imagine yourself standing in the same place: Only this time, before you get to shoot your first arrow, someone puts a blindfold over your eyes and spins you around several times. Although you know the target is out there somewhere, you will be forced to shoot your arrows in the general direction where you thought the target was located before you were spun around. Not only are you unable to see the target, you can't see where your arrows are going, so you can't make any worthwhile adjustments. Your chances of hitting the target have been greatly reduced by one simple factor: you can't see the target. All you can hope to do is to get lucky. All of the other factors remained exactly the same: you still have the same bow, the same number of arrows, and the same distance to the target. This one factor, namely being able to clearly identify the target, has made all the difference in the world.

Many people set goals but are not achieving them. Why do you think this is so?

Think about how the word goal is used in our society. We describe it as something to work toward. That description implies that your objective will be difficult to achieve – which carries with it an implied message that it is just as likely as not that the ultimate goal will not be achieved. By describing the thing we want as a goal, we have created a situation in which our mind already knows it will be difficult to accomplish, and, at least in most circumstance, okay (or at least forgivable) if we fail. Goals are like New Year's resolutions… frequently made and rarely accomplished. Take a moment and think about all the goals you have ever heard that others have set for themselves. Once you have that picture in your mind, ask yourself how many of those goals – yours and others – were actually reached. The answer usually is "not very many". If that is true (and it always is), then think of what the word goal has come to mean to you. It has come to mean that a goal is something you should try hard to achieve because it would be fun or good to have, but most of the time, goals aren't really achieved.

Why do we have to be more specific when it comes to goal setting?

When I have asked some people to identify their promise, they respond with answers like, "I want to be famous", or "I want to make a lot of money and have a lot of fun". When I hear descriptions like this, I then ask: "How rich? "How famous?" "How much money is a 'lot'?" "What is 'fun'?"

Almost always, my question is met with a blank look on the person's face. Very few people have a reply. Some people attempt a reply with whatever comes to mind – and it is obvious to both of us that up to that moment in time, they had never really tried to clearly identify what they think they want. Like the "pin the tail on the donkey" game or the archery example I used, unless you can specifically answer this question, you really don't even have a target to shoot at.

If you want to achieve an objective, you also must have clearly identified target. The narrower and the more specific you can make your promise, the better. For example:

An average golfer will aim for the green. A professional golfer will aim for the flag.

Mel Gibson, in the movie *The Patriot*, tells his son, "Aim small – miss small." The corollary to Mel's advice is: if you aim big, you may miss big.

How can we deal with challenges along the way in pursuing your goals?

The most common cause of failing to achieve a stated objective is the inability to deal with self-doubt. When we first embark on the path to achieve a new objective, we are excited and charged up. We are truly and fully motivated. We see feel the target toward which we are striving and have all the confidence in the world that we will achieve our ambition. Thereafter (and sometimes, only shortly thereafter), we begin to lose this emotional excitement and realize we are going to have to work hard to accomplish this goal.

Think of a person whose name can invoke wither a positive or negative image in your mind. You can strive for an objective in order to please someone or, in the alternative, to show someone. When you think of your promise, who is the person you are doing it for? Who is the person you want to show you can do this? Although a book on positive thinking will rarely extol the virtues of negative thinking, there are occasions when a negative personal motivator will help you accomplish a positive objective.

Identifying a personal motivator will provide an emotional reaction and additional energy to help you accomplish your promise. Both of these will be especially helpful during any frustration cycles you might encounter. If you can identify more than one personal motivator, that is all the better, the more reason you have for wanting to accomplish this promise, the easier it will be for you to stay focused on the target.

Think of a lesson that you learned the hard way about how to live a successful and happy life?

Back when I was a teenager, my present wife Kathy and I were dating and I suffered from very low self-esteem. I would constantly refer to myself as a bum and good for nothing, and so on, because that's all I had heard up to that point in my life.

One day, while I was driving Kathy to work, I was telling her that I didn't know what she saw in me, or why she even liked me, and her response was screaming, "Stop this car and let me out!" Scared out of my wits, I pulled the car over immediately, and she got out. I asked, "What's wrong?" Kathy said, "If you're going to keep saying those things about yourself, then I don't want to have anything to do with you. I don't see you the way you see yourself, but if you can't understand that and change your attitude about yourself, we're through."

Well, I loved Kathy and knew that I wanted to marry her, so I promised I would change, and I did. My attitude about myself improved. I realized that I was worthy of Kathy and of who I was. My self-esteem improved 100 percent. I learned that I could do anything

I set my mind to, and that's when I decided to get my GED and pursue a college education. Kathy became a positive motivator in my life, and I'm grateful, even still today.

Why do we need a plan in whatever we do?

Every successful business has a written business plan. I realize this is a universal statement because I used the word "every" in the sentence. I am very aware that it is exceedingly rare that any universal statement is always accurate. I am, however, willing to wager that this is one of those rare times when a universal statement is true. In my 40 years of doing business in the USA and abroad, in all of my dealings from Wall Street to Silicon Valley to Main Street America, and from my experience with small businesses to billion-dollar-a-year businesses, I have never come across a successful business that didn't have a well-thought-out business plan.

The mere creating, writing, and reviewing of a business plan helps the businessperson understand clearly where he or she is going, how to get there, when it will happen, who will be needed along the way, what it will take, and what the reward will be when the objective is met. Now, aren't those the very same questions you will need to know about your promise – if you hope to achieve it?

Why is it important to write down the plan?

The first reason is that an objective created in your mind is "thought". Our brain processes "thought" the same way it does information provided by our senses; the more we can reinforce (identify) this objective in our brain, the clearer the target will be. The mere act of writing it out will cause you to focus on the promise. It also allows your outer senses to become involved as we use touch to write and sight to see and record this target you have set for yourself. The human mind receives its information from our various senses. The more senses we can involve in identifying our objective, the more assistance the mind can and will provide.

The second reason you must write it down is that the mere exercise of writing it down will require you to clarify not only the objective but also other things that will be crucial if you are to succeed in your quest.

While it is important to write it down, simply writing it down as a statement is not enough. We need to show our mind how we are going to accomplish this objective. Remember, the mind will not allow us to do something it thinks we cannot do (it wants to save us from the embarrassment and humiliation of failure), and conversely, our mind will allow (and help) us to do those things it thinks we are capable of accomplishing. So if we want to prevent our mind from frustrating our attempt – and at the same time we want to create an environment in which our mind will help us accomplish our objective – we need to persuade our mind that we can do whatever it is we have set down as our objective.

Why is it important to review our goals on a regular basis?

Once you have created your promise plan, now put your plan where you will see it on a regular basis. Some people put their promise plan with their checkbook or their stack of household bills waiting to be paid. By doing so, they know that they will both touch and see their promise plan at least once a month, if not more often. Since the promise plan is the detailed business plan of what, how, when, where, and why, as we review it from time to time, we have the opportunity to revise anything that needs revision.

I have my promise plan in the front pocket of a notebook I carry with me every day. I don't look at it every day, but I do pull it out at least once every week to see if I am on track and on schedule. I make at least some minor revision every time I review it. There are occasions when something new has happened or new information has come to my attention that causes me to make a major or minor revision.

Can you share with us a goal-tracking tool we can use on a daily basis?

A visual reminder is anything that will remind you or motivate you to work to accomplish your promise. Put your visual reminder in a place where you will have to see it daily. Find the location suited to you where you will see it most often. Put reminders of your promise in many locations throughout your home or office. Visual reminders are limited only by our imagination. For example you can use an index card that contains the name of your personal motivator (positive or negative), or anything else you choose to write – so long as your reaction to it will be motivational. You can put this index card in a wide range of locations – you decide what's best:

The bathroom mirror, so you see it every morning as you get ready for work.

The bedroom wall, as I did with the note card with my sister-in-law's name, so that I could see it every time I got up from my study desk.

The wall of your office or work cubicle, so you are reminded of it frequently during the course of your workday.

What is a mastermind group? Why would it be beneficial to form such an alliance?

Napoleon Hill, in this classic self-help book entitled "Think and Grow Rich", introduced the world to the term "mastermind". Napoleon Hill tells the story of how Henry Ford, Thomas Edison, Harvey Firestone, and a handful of other very successful and prominent businessman of the late eighteenth and early nineteenth centuries would gather on a regular occasion to help each other with their respective business issues. During these sessions, one of the members would identify their particular problem or issue. During the balance of the session, all the participants would offer their advice and recommendation on how to accomplish the task and solve the problem. Napoleon Hill termed this process the "mastermind" because the solution that flows from the process was not just the product of one mind but rather the mind of all those in attendance.

Hill went on to explain that the power wasn't just because these were all very, very smart businessman. It was something more than that. By all of them working together in a concert with a mutual objective of helping each other, they created a process that produced results that not one of them alone could have produced. This is a classic example of where "the whole becomes greater than the sum of the parts".

Some people might shy away from the term "mastermind" under the mistaken belief that it implies something mystical, which it does not. The modern-day version of this same process is frequently referred to as a "board of advisors."

How do we start a mastermind group?

Identify a small group of people who have demonstrated the qualities you admire. Arrange a personal visit with each, and at this meeting, explain your promise and ask if he or she would be willing to meet with you and a few others one night (day) a month for a few hours. At the first meeting, show the individual your promise plan to demonstrate your sincerity and commitment to the process. You will be amazed by the helpful response you receive.

I have utilized this concept in every business venture in which I have been engaged over the past forty years. It has produced tremendous results for me. By sharing my problems and concerns with people who have remarkably different backgrounds and different areas of expertise, I have been able to tap into ideas and solutions that I would have been incapable of accomplishing by myself.

CHAPTER 6

Ancient Eastern wisdom for today's world

Chin-Ning Chu – Strategist

> The world consists of a delicate balance of two great opposing forces. Asian philosophy refers to them as Yin and Yang. All things are composed of these two forces.

Biography

Chin-Ning Chu is a descendant of the pauper who became the first Emperor of the Ming Dynasty. At the age of three, Chin-Ning was forced to leave behind her family's fortune and flee to Taiwan as a refugee. At the age of ten, her father began to teach her strategies by reading the text of the ancient Chinese art of war classics as bedtime stories. At the age of 22, clutching two suitcases, again, she left home to come to America, struggling with a new language and culture. Chin-Ning is one of the foremost speakers on the practical application of *Sun Tzu's Art of War* and a promoter of strategic thinking as the core competency among leaders of government and corporations worldwide. She collaborated with Discovery Television and the US Library of Congress on the production of their Great Books Series: *Sun Tzu's Art of War.*

Chin-Ning is a number one best-selling author throughout Asia and Australia where her books have out-sold those of Hillary Clinton and Tony Robbins. Her books: *The Art of War for Women; Thick Face, Black Heart; Do Less, Achieve More;* and *The Asian Mind Game* have been translated into 25 languages with readers in over 60 countries. Her readers include a number of influential political and business leaders.

Her work is highly praised by the media across five continents including *USA Today, Business Week,* the United Kingdom's *Financial Times,* China's *People Daily,* Australia's *Financial Review* and Brazil's *ISTO E.* When the world encountered collisions such as the caning incident in Singapore, CNN's CrossFire turned to Chin-Ning for understanding.

Chin-Ning's name was listed among the all-time Successful Writers by the prominent British/US publisher, Nicholas Brealey Publishing. On the cover of the book "50 Success Classics," Chin-Ning Chu is presented with such notables as Benjamin Franklin, Napoleon Hill, Sun Tzu and Andrew Carnegie.

How did you start out? What early experiences shaped the person you are today?

In 1949, at the age of three, holding tight onto my mother's skirt, I ran with my parents and two young brothers across a Shanghai airport runway. Amid the sound of bombs blasting, we boarded the last commercial flight out of China. From a life of affluence and privilege, my family was reduced to the condition of faceless immigrants among millions in Taiwan who had fled the conquering Communists. All the possessions we were able to salvage from the devastation of our lives fitted into the suitcases my parent carried.

In 1969, when I was 22, I left Taiwan to begin a new life in America. Once more a faceless immigrant, I arrived in Los Angeles with two suitcases containing the few possessions I was able to bring to my new home: clothes I had made for myself, a few personal effects, and two books. By this time, I had already read hundreds of books, and I owned many; I brought only two to USA: *Sun Tzu's Art of War* and a slim, black-bound volume written by Lee Zhong Wu called *Thick Black Theory*. Although I cannot say exactly why I brought *Thick Black Theory* with me, at the time I had a strong, intuitive sense that it would prove to be very important.

Having been raised in China, I was already immersed in Buddhism, Taoism, and Confucianism, despite the fact that I was Catholic. My continued search for understanding took me to all parts of the world. I studied the Hindu scriptures and Christian mystics. At one point, I gave up my successful business career in Los Angeles and moved to a remote mountain in the Oregon Cascades for a long period of meditation and soul-searching. As my horizon broadened, I came back to my Chinese roots with a new perspective. I looked at Buddhism, Taoism, Confucianism, and their Japanese extraction, Zen Buddhism. It became clear to me that these diverse religions and philosophies shared the same central principle and that if I could understand and extract this principle, it would give me the power and control over my own life that I sought.

For years I tried, without success, to write *Thick Black Theory*. Finally, I turned away from it and wrote my first two books, *The Chinese Mind Game* and *The Asian Mind Game*. Later I wrote *Thick Face Black Heart* and it became an international bestseller with readers in over 60 countries.

Ancient Chinese philosophy emphasizes the importance of attuning to the rhythm of nature for success.
Can you elaborate on what this means?

The world consists of a delicate balance of two great opposing forces. Asian philosophy refers to them as Yin and Yang. All things are composed of these two forces. Things that are thought to be opposite are more intimately related than is commonly believed. Opposites are not two entities that balance each other. They are, in reality, two aspects of the same thing. Darkness cannot exist without light, nor good without evil. Violence and nonviolence arise out of the same place in the human soul.

Just as there are two aspects to all things, there are two aspects to human actions: the inward motivation and the outward appearance. Without considering the inward motivation, it is impossible to us to judge our actions or the actions of the others. The sage and the criminal might commit the same crime against the state out of entirely different motives. Christ was crucified between two thieves because those who stood in judgment of him saw no great difference between his actions and those of two petty criminals.

You need to understand that you possess creative and destructive forces in equal measure. Both complement each other and cannot be judged by common standards of good and evil. Each has its proper time. It is part of understanding yourself and your destiny to know when to exercise your destructive force and when to submit to the destructive force of others. The grass bends easily in the wind. The great oak stands unmoved. A strong wind can uproot the oak, but no winds, however strong, can uproot the grass that bends flat before it.

In our practical daily lives, how can we go with the flow of life rather than work against it?

Today in our society, it is vital to exhibit your sense of self-confidence. It is a delight to watch people who are absolutely secure with themselves. However, if you are not among them, don't lose heart. I'm going to reveal one of the greatest secrets: only fools and saints are totally and absolutely secure about themselves. The rest of the world is faking it to certain degrees, and some are better fakers than others. We often blame our negativity as the cause of our failure in our work. In fact, the source of our problem is not our negativities, but rather that we have chosen uninspiring tasks that bring forth our negativities.

Recently, I was with my partner doing a patent search for our new invention. As I was doing the work, I found that I was very negative toward the whole process of the search. I felt ashamed of my selfishness and unwillingness to help. I asked myself why I was behaving this way. Then I realized that it was not because I was negative and unwilling to do the work. I was willing to work, but I just didn't want to do that kind of work. I couldn't stand being in that patent office doing repetitive, numerical, rule-following tasks, which I have always hated.

My conclusion was that I am neither lazy nor selfish. When I perform work that is suited to my nature, the job will be effortless and even inspiring. I finally paid the attorney to do the search.

Whatever your negativity is, make it pay for itself. If your negativity is that you love to sit and do nothing but read, find out how you can read all day and get paid for it; perhaps find a job at a publishing company or library, or be a book critic. If your negativity is a love of eating, find out how you can get a job centered around food. Maybe you can be a chef or write a food column. If your negativity is a love of watching movies, turn the world upside down and find out how you can make a living in the movie business. If you cannot find an occupation centered around your favorite "negativity," create a job that no one else has thought about.

You teach that the secret to personal transformation starts from within. How will this accelerate our path to abundance and success?

The famous book *Think and Grow Rich* teaches us how we can think ourselves to riches. Throughout the years, I have carefully observed how people obtained wealth. It is not thinking, reading, or listening that transfers us from poverty to wealth. Rather, it is a switch of attitude from the center of our being. You can think all you want, you can affirm all you want, you can understand all you can possibly understand, but it will not necessarily change you or your circumstances.

There is another aspect to this mysterious puzzle. You need to perceive yourself as being successful and then operate your life as if you were. It is essential to uproot from your consciousness thoughts that somehow you are lacking and unworthy. Operate from abundance and self-importance. To some this comes naturally; others have to work consciously at it. When Grace Kelly first appeared in

Hollywood, she was nobody, but she carried herself naturally, as if she already were a great star. When she actually was a great star, she looked and acted more like a princess than a movie star.

Your circumstances will not change until your knowledge and your understanding takes on a living form from within. Because you have transformed, suddenly everything becomes possible. This transformation has no fixed formula. It results from your willingness to battle within and your unceasing courage to cultivate your inner strength to overcome your liabilities. Through this self-cultivation, you will eventually produce the magical fruit that will transform your attitudes in every aspect of your life. Before you can garner the external rewards you first must inwardly experience that they already belong to you. In short, your inner reality will take the form of a self-fulfilling prophecy. Your actions will be unforced and much more effective because they are motivated from within, not because you are mechanically following a formula. Outer success will follow the actions and attitudes you manifest due to your experience of success as an inner reality.

How can we deal with life's challenges gracefully and make peace with ourselves?

I have seen many people grow old, but not graciously. Their eyes reflect pain and disillusionment. They have been beaten by life; they have so many unbroken dreams. The hope and expectation of youth have vanished – only death awaits. The mistake they made was not preparing themselves for the harsh lessons their Creator set for them on life's path – necessary lessons to strengthen their spirit and make them fit for greatness. Unlike the warrior who accepts harsh discipline as a privilege and honor, these people are pieces of grain caught in the millstone, ground down by the wheel of life, in agony and in pain.

As most do, I used to pray for good times and good fortune. The prayer "Let thy will be done" used to scare me to death. In reality, though, this world in which we live is fragmented and ever-changing, and our existence and survival are delicately connected to the invisible thread of God's grace. Gain and loss are the constant human conditions. Now when I pray, I pray for the unshakable inner strength and the strength of the warrior to accept these harsh lessons and learn from them, rather than be destroyed by them.

To become successful in life, why is it important to balance optimism with realistic expectations?

When I was younger, I used to be obsessed with optimism. I could not tolerate any thought of a possible ill outcome. If anyone even suggested that I should weigh the worst-case scenarios with the best-case scenarios, I was offended. The truth is, I was too scared to examine "real life". Instead, I lived in the world of "make believe". It is good to have a positive attitude because it allows you to see everything as within your reach. The possibility of ill fate or bad luck becomes the sole property of those people who think negatively. Now, I realized that being realistic is not being negative. It is positive. It is not because of negativity that a cruise ship captain educates his passengers on how to behave in an emergency. He doesn't plan on having the ship sink. He is merely realistic and prepared.

Often, the so-called "negative" people are the most realistic. Being overly optimistic sometimes can be a liability in the real world. A CEO cannot afford the luxury of excessive optimism, because it will lead him to failure – just as an overly optimistic general who becomes careless will underestimate his battlefield foe and lead his troop to their demise. The result can be costly. Similarly, the coach and the quarterback shouldn't adopt the cheerleader's ardent enthusiasm. If the coach and the quarterback fail to realistically size up the opposing team's strengths, their positive thinking alone will not assure them victory.

A realistic person tends to forecast potential problems and anticipate difficulties ahead. The Texas oil entrepreneur T. Boone Pickens, Jr. explains that the shortcoming of most geologists is that they are too optimistic. As an independent oilman without the backing of huge conglomerates, he has to be much more pragmatic about his drilling ventures. Gilbert, a vice president in charge of commercial loans at a major bank, told me that he preferred working with the realistic borrowers as opposed to the overly enthusiastic ones. The realistic borrower understands the potential difficulties and is prepare to ride the waves of challenge, while an overly enthusiastic borrower tends to underestimate the actualities of starting or expanding a business.

You likened the ancient Eastern concept of Dharma to a wish-fulfilling tree.
What is Dharma?

The word Dharma comes from Sanskrit, the oldest language in the world, which originated in ancient India. It has been confirmed by leading Western linguists that Sanskrit is the root of virtually all known languages. Dharma came from the word *dhar*, which means to "support, uphold, and nourish Dharma is the understanding of appropriate action for any given circumstance. It means "to act in accordance with one's duty." Each person, depending on his station in life, will have different Dharma. For example, a warrior's Dharma is to slay his nation's enemies. A physician's Dharma is to save lives. If Dharma is followed, the world will be in harmony with the natural law.

People who practice Dharma accept life as it comes and perform their duty accordingly. Dharma is the natural law that guides us to recognize at any moment the role that each one of us is playing in life. Being true to the duty of that particular role at any given time and the very act of accepting and performing that action to the best of our ability – that is following Dharma.

Most of us struggle and work hard at pursuing our goals.
How did you learn to relax and allow your Dharma to unfold effortlessly?

If you feel you are stuck in your work right now, whatever it is, keep on doing it with dedication and devotion. You were not placed in that position entirely by accident. There are lessons there for you to learn. Your total commitment to your present work and the experience you accumulate can serve as a springboard for the unfolding of your greater destiny. Take me, for example, I had been a consultant for US companies and individuals who were doing or wish to do business with Asians. I liked my work but always felt there was something missing. Yet I performed my work faithfully. Only by doing so was I able to discover what was missing in my work: the satisfaction I could gain from my ability to reach large numbers of people and inspire their thinking.

By continuing to perform my work, and through my experience of doing business in Asia, I realized that there was a need for Americans, in their business dealings, to understand the Asian mind in depth. It was then I saw that the way to reach and inspire large numbers of people would be through writing a book about this very issue. Accordingly, I wrote about the Asian mindset in business dealings with Westerners. The success of the book led to great personal satisfaction. I went on to write more books, expanding the topic. Years later, I realized I did not have to write only about Asian business strategies. There was an abundance of rich wisdom from the Orient that I could communicate to Western readers. Thus I wrote the book *Thick Face Black Heart* and it became an international bestseller.

By simply being aware that there is a Divine plan for your life that awaits to unfold in the course of life itself, you will begin to be consciously in tune with every incident that comes into your professional and personal life. Treat each incident with the eye of a good detective and try to unveil the mystery of your fate. This is the first and the most essential Dharma in discovering your destiny and your life path.

When we are in challenging and difficult situations, how will understanding our Dharma lead to a successful outcome?

I myself had a profound experience while traveling in Taiwan on business. One of my objectives there was to represent a US firm on a visit to the firm's Taiwan representative. The Taiwan company had been doing a very poor job of selling the US company's product.

I spent a long time rehearsing in my mind how I should approach the Taiwan company. Should I be casual and friendly or take a more official stand to find out why their sales performance had been so poor? I went through many ways to open the conversation, but none felt right. The problem was the Taiwan company's owner was a dear friend of mine. Being heavy-handed or coming to him with a very light touch seemed equally inappropriate. During my self inquiry, I was undecided.

I asked myself, what is the Dharma in this situation? I then realized the only proper way to approach the Taiwan company was to be open and direct and to find out how I (representing the US company's interest) could better serve them. I should find out what their difficulties were and how I could help. If I supported them in doing their job better, they would be turn do a better job for my US client. As soon as I realized what my Dharma was in this circumstance, I felt totally open and positive toward these people. I no longer had to rehearse how to speak to them. Since I now had a proper attitude toward the situation, the words that came out of my mouth could only be right.

What are the important factors of the Dharma of self-effort?

Success comes in every shape and profile. Countless good books have been published in this subject. All this information can contribute to our effort towards success, but the truth remains – success has no rules. Success comes to some of the most negative people as well as the most positive ones. Success comes to those who try hard and even to those who make no visible effort.

1. Quest for harmony; self-effort does not mean blind effort. The Dharma of self-effort also includes striving to know when to exercise the discrimination of acceptance and surrender to a disappointing outcome. However, this does not mean giving up, but rather finding harmony within oneself in order to gather the necessary strength and move on to the next level of life.

2. Tenacious determination: the American cartoonist and creator of "Pogo," Walt Kelly, often said, "We have seen the enemy, and he is us." In the battle of life, you are the enemy, and you are the warrior. In the battle of life, as

long as you are fighting, you are winning. Each day, if you fail a hundred times but win once, that single win will strengthen you and provide you with the strength for the next win. Never let go of your fight.

3. There is no quitting: life is a school. This school does not give out passing grades, but demands a perfect A from every student on every subject. You can never quit this school and this school has no time limit for graduation. However, as long as you are fighting the battle tenaciously and courageously, the magical, unseen hand of the Divine is there to aid. This is not merely rhetoric, but a common experience that many people have found to be true.

4. All good things come to those who strive with patience: our sense of self-limitation did not form overnight. Thus, we require patience to readjust our course. A good phrase from the ancient Chinese elucidates this point: "Dripping water, in time, will cut a hole through the stone." When we were infants, like bees, we were in tune with our natural instincts. If you have self-determination and self-effort, no one can keep you from manifesting your true destiny, the mystery of a towering fruit tree lies dormant within a tiny seed.

How can we learn to be more patient with our everyday life and work?

All of my life I have been a champion of self-effort. Sometimes my self-effort paid off and other times the results were meager, but nothing has affected me so fundamentally as the experience of a recent event.

When I was writing my last book, I had done everything right. I worked overtime to get my finished work to the publisher on time. I had successfully obtained an endorsement from Texas oilman, T. Boone Pickens, Jr., in addition to one from an editor of *USA today*. The book was scheduled to be published at a specific time. Then came Operation Desert Storm in January. All the media's attention turned to the war, and my book missed the opportunity for its grand entrance. Nevertheless, I learned an invaluable lesson. If I had not pushed myself and my editor to the limit in order to get the work done, if I had been late in turning in my manuscript, things might have worked out better.

When things don't turn out as expected, it may be a blessing in disguised. Now, after I have done my best, I relax and watch to see the outcome. Deep down at an unseen level, I know I will never be the same again. To others, I may not look any different, but I know I have gained a unique insight into the Dharma of acceptance and surrender.

Many people do not enjoy the work they do. What is your advice to them?

Work is a primary method used to express ourselves in fulfilling our obligations to support ourselves. Through work, we contribute to the collective good of society and the evolution of man. There is no division between your daily work and your spiritual unfoldment. Every situation will accelerate your spiritual evolution. Your work is where your spiritual unfoldment takes place.

Through work, we encounter people and events that mirror our spiritual state. Through work, people and events either irritate us or uplift us. Whether it is irritation or inspiration, the universal intention is to utilize that particular situation to teach us a beneficial lesson. Nothing in life happens by accident. If people and events in your life stir strong emotions, it signals the need to take a good look at yourself in that area. For example, every time I write a book, I learn much more about the subject than I initially dreamed possible.

Many great figures, whether in business, sport, or politics, talk about using intuition as a tool for better decision making. What is your view on this?

The definition of intuition according to the dictionary is as follows:

1. Direct perception of truths, facts, etc., independently of any reasoning process.

2. Pure, untaught, noninferential knowledge.

Intuition is a commodity that is extremely undervalued in the Western world, yet everyone who has ever succeeded in any extraordinary task has always drawn upon this power. A good trial attorney must be well versed in law and should research his case. However, he or she also needs to perceive intuitively the minds of the jury so that his presentation will sway the jury members in favor of his client.

I was told by a homicide detective that a good detective understands how to follow instincts and gut feeling, whether seemingly on the right track or not. A good business man or woman, after examining available data, ultimately will have to rely on gut feelings to make the final decision. Many revolutionary scientific breakthroughs often begin with an intuitive perception of unknown potential by a scientist. The scientist then proceeds to prove his intuition through scientific experimentation and conclusions. At the age of sixteen, Albert Einstein asked, "If I moved at the speed of light, what would light look like?" This question was the seed for his theory of relativity, which he spent the rest of his life trying to explain to the world.

Many people are confronted by fears when it comes to pursuing the things they want, whether in their own life, that of their family, or in their work/career. How can we attain mastery over the emotion of fear?

Fear is the most destructive of emotions. Fear is to a man's soul as a drop of poison is to a well of spring water. Fear wears so many masks and comes in so many forms. Deep down in our subconscious, we are wise enough to recognize the fragility of how this universe was put together; that our existence and survival hang on the invisible thread of God's grace. In our conscious awareness, fear is a vague but constantly nagging uneasiness. Most people do not even know that they are afraid most of the time.

Years ago, I decided to organize and conduct a full-day seminar about how to do business with Asians. The morning of the seminar, while I was dressing, I was overwhelmed by fear. Suddenly it hit me: I had never spoken in front of any large groups. What if I opened my mouth and nothing came out? What would this do to my professional reputation? How would I get through this day? In that instant, I had envisioned the entire day and was convinced I would fail and be devastated.

As I was driving toward the hotel, I thought to myself, "I either shape up or admit defeat." I decided the only way I could get rid of my fear was to stop wanting to avoid the feelings of being fearful. To stop resisting it. The more I did not want to feel fearful, the more intense the fear got. I mentally took my fear from my heart, placed it in front of me on my dashboard, and started to stare into this fear with great intensity. I said to myself, "Let me be more fierce than fear itself." Suddenly the fear I had been feeling was replaced by the intense courage that I had created by staring at the fear. By the time I arrived at the hotel, I was charged with power and enthusiasm. My first seminar was a great success. After I had finished at 4:00 p.m., no one wanted to leave – they wanted to hear more! My experience was not extraordinary. Often the bravest warriors were originally the greatest cowards. The more fear you confront and conquer the greater courage you will possess.

There is a famous saying, "The only thing we have to fear is fear itself". What is your view on this statement?

For most of us, fear is not grounded in any real possibilities of catastrophe; rather, it is a state of emotional uneasiness. Mark Twain clearly understood this well when he said that most of our worries and fears never came true. Don't give your fear too much importance. An ignored guest often departs unannounced. Wherever we turn, we are face to face with different aspects of fear. It is the biggest barrier for us to overcome in order to experience and fulfill our true potential. To overcome fear, first you have to find the courage and will to confront it. Fear is never so terrifying once you look into its eyes. If you are not concerned about the outcome of a circumstance, you will experience no fear. When you attach yourself to expectations, anxiety and fear will overcome you. The outcome will be what it will be, regardless of your expectations and fears.

CHAPTER 7

High performance in a demanding world

Siimon Reynolds – High Achievement Expert

> *How big should your goals be? Well, they need to be grand enough to excite you, yet realistic enough that you believe you can reach them. I like Brian Tracy's rule of thumb: you should feel as though you have a 50% chance of reaching your goal.*

Biography

A renowned Australian entrepreneur, Siimon Reynolds has been a dominant force in the advertising industry for over 25 years. He is the co-founder of Photon Group, which in just over eight years has grown from zero to 54 marketing companies in 14 countries, employing over 6,000 full and part-time staff. Photon Group has been listed on the Australian Stock Exchange since 2004, and according to *Advertising Age* was the 15th largest marketing group in the world and the world's fastest growing marketing group in 2008. He is currently Chairman and co-founder of OMG, Australia's largest online network, currently developing over 30,000 websites.

Siimon has won almost every major advertising award for creativity in the world, including the *Gold Lion at Cannes, the Gold Pencil at the New York One Show awards* and *The Grand Prix at the London International Advertising Awards*. His Australian awards include *Television Commercial of the Year, Magazine Ad of the Year, Newspaper Ad of the Year* and *Agency of the Year,* twice. Siimon is also winner of the *NSW Young Achiever of the Year*, Career section.

Siimon now speaks internationally on success and human achievement. He recently appeared on the TV show *Dragon's Den,* as one of Australia's most successful entrepreneurs. He also coaches a small number of senior executives and entrepreneurs on how to maximize their performance, make more profits, and live a more balanced life. His latest book, *Why People Fail: The 15 Biggest Obstacles to Success and How You Can Beat Them* will be published worldwide in 2010. He has been featured on *60 Minutes, Today Tonight, A Current Affair, Bloomberg* and America's *NBC The Today Show*.

How did you start out? What early experiences shaped the person you are today?

Originally, I went into advertising as a writer, simply because it seemed a good way to make money without going to university! But I soon became excited by the creative potential of advertising: While the majority of advertisements are boring and crass, a handful are absolutely magnificent. Once I decided to try and create the latter, my career really took off. I truly believe – as the great football coach Vince Lombardi used to say – "The quality of a person's life is in direct proportion to their commitment to excellence, regardless of their chosen field of endeavor".

The moment I started aiming for greatness, my life began to change for the better. After opening and growing several advertising agencies, I eventually co-founded Photon Group, which now operates in 14 countries and consists of over 50 companies, employing over 6000 people.

In answer to how I got here, I would have to say I did three important things as a 19-year-old: I aimed high, I forced myself to become excellent at my craft, and I chose to believe I could make it.

What is the best way to find your purpose in life?

Well firstly I would suggest setting a deadline for choosing your purpose; whether it's a week, a month or a year. The reason I say that is I've met so many people who wander through life thinking about what their purpose is for decades, and end up trapped in an endless holding pattern of indecision.

That's no way to live. Better to just choose a purpose, give it 100 percent, and make it into a masterpiece. Don't wait for some divine inspiration. Find something you enjoy and resolve to master it – even if it takes ten years. Once you commit fully to any goal, your passion for it will massively increase.

A Harvard study conducted by Professor Edward Banfield, found that the most important determinant of success was cultivating a long-term time perspective. So once you've chosen your purpose, be mentally prepared to focus on it for the long term, rather than chopping and changing your mind about it. An average person who commits and focuses his or her mind will outperform a genius who is ever-changing and uncommitted, every time.

How do you define genuine success?

Success is all about progressing toward worthwhile goals. But those goals need to be holistic in nature. If you are making progress toward your selected physical, mental, spiritual, career, and relationship goals, then you will be uncommonly successful. If you only excel in one of those arenas, however, then genuine success and certainly authentic happiness will elude you.

Too often our society worships someone who is excellent in only one area, yet may be performing terribly in all the others. That may be focus, but it isn't genuine success.

Of course, holistic success takes very careful time management and organizational skills, just to get everything done. Few people treat these skills seriously, and they soon find they don't have nearly enough time to make substantial progress on all of their goals. The cold, hard truth is there are always two aspects to achieving anything: The goal itself, and organizing yourself so that you can be highly productive in achieving it. Fortunately, time management is a science, with many effective techniques developed over centuries. It's a science well worth mastering if you aim to be truly and holistically successful.

What do you consider to be the secret of happiness?

For most of the last century, psychiatry focused on making sick people normal, rather than making normal people happy. Until the mid 1980s, there was very little research on what actually made humans feel great. Then came the birth of a new scientific field, Positive Psychology, and research into happiness really blossomed.

In the last 20 years there's been a huge amount of research done on happiness by eminent scientists like Ed Diener, Martin Seligman, Tim Kasser, and Mihaly Csikzentmihalyi. In summary, to be happy we need several close personal relationships, an optimistic thinking style, reasonable control over our environment, a sense of purpose or meaning, a job that involves us deeply, and relatively low stress levels.

Contrary to popular opinion, there is very little correlation between wealth and happiness. In fact, a study showed that members of the "Forbes 400" list of richest Americans are only on average one percent happier than the average wage earner.

How can one become great in one's field?

It's simple to become outstanding in your field, but it's certainly not easy.

Firstly, do something you enjoy. That way long hours won't bother you. The truth is that even if you work really hard in a field, if you're not really into it your results will never be superlative.

Next, dedicate yourself to continuous study in your area. Almost nobody does this. So many people stop studying their field the moment they graduate from their first course in it.

Third, find role models – people who have achieved excellence in your field – and copy what they do. Better yet, ask them to mentor you. You can literally cut 20 years off your career learning curve if you follow the right role model.

Finally, maintain a philosophy of excellence every day by holding yourself to a world class standard. By simply dedicating yourself to always doing the best you can every day, you will soon shine far brighter than your competitors.

If you do only one of these, you will still be more successful than most people. But do all of them and you will become a legend in your field.

Basically becoming great at anything is all about deliberate practice, and incremental improvement. As Geoff Colvin proved in his outstanding book, *Talent Is Overrated*, hard work and dedication applied over many years beats natural talent every time. Society believes the opposite: that it's the naturally talented who usually win. Colvin's research proves that this simply isn't true.

What are the personal qualities of top achievers?

There are many. But at the very least, top achievers see themselves as being superb, even before they are. They have strong positive self concepts. They also continually refine their skills, even after twenty years on the job. (Most people stop trying to get better at their work after the age of thirty).

Generally, superlative performers also have the ability to get on with people. Very few can make it to the top without enlisting help from others around them. Daniel Goleman's work on Emotional Intelligence showed that people with strong EQ (ability to get on with others, self discipline, positive thinking, etc.) were around twice as likely to be successful than people who had just a high IQ.

Add strong dose of passion and that pretty much sums up the characteristics of top performers, regardless of their profession. It's important to realize that most of these winning character traits can be developed with focus, willpower, and dedication.

How can we cultivate more fun, joy and laughter in our lives?

Joy is a choice – it really is. It's not about having everything in life going perfectly. There are people who are happy even though their daily lives are immensely tough. Take a look at some African tribal people, as an example. Many of them are beaming with happiness even though they have so little.

The truth is, when you decide to be happy – no matter what your circumstances are – then you will become happier almost immediately. As Dr. Robert Holden's studies have shown, you don't need a reason to be happy, just choosing to be so will soon fill your life with joy, almost regardless of how many challenges you may be facing. As Buddha said, "Nothing is, but thinking makes it so". If you wait for all the circumstances in your life to be great before you allow yourself to be happy, you will be waiting for most of your life.

In addition, I have found that if you force yourself to act happy, within a few minutes your mood will improve. The founders of Neuro Linguistic Programming, Grinder and Bandler, have done some excellent research on this.

What is the key thinking that separates the average from the great?

It may seem simplistic, but in reality there is only one difference between the thinking of the greats versus the average. The great ones have a huge desire to be great, while mediocre people have weak desire, or none at all. That overwhelming desire for excellence then affects their entire performance: how they think day to day, the actions they take, who they associate with, and therefore all their results. So it all stems from that original burning desire.

In addition, I believe that white-hot desire magnetically attracts opportunities and luck into your life. While we may never be able to prove that, I know many highly successful people who are living proof that it's true.

It's worthwhile to monitor your desire level every month. For example, on the first day of each month you can set up a diary reminder so you can rate your achievement desire level on a scale of 1–10, and then never accept less than a score of 8. You can have tremendous talent, but without a strong desire to accompany it, true greatness will be elusive.

How do we maintain inner balance?

Self awareness is key. If you wish to maintain inner balance, you must set this as a daily goal in order to remain conscious of it. Once you are thinking about it much of the day, you will automatically see ways to maintain your inner balance. Mind and medicine guru Dr. Deepak Chopra suggests thinking of one positive word, like 'happy', all day long. Simply by being conscious of the word happy, our happiness usually increases. In life we tend to get what we think about.

Once you've set inner balance as a goal, rituals and systems need to be developed to keep you on track. For example, if you had a daily ritual of 20 minutes meditation, 20 minutes exercise and 20 minutes reading from inspirational or spiritual books, you would soon find your inner balance will dramatically increase. But without a daily system and ritual, it's very easy to get caught up with life's daily traumas and tribulations and forget about your goal of creating inner balance. The other key is to visualize yourself as being balanced. After a while, you will start acting in accordance with that vision. We usually perform according to the self image we have of ourselves, deep down inside.

What is the best way to set goals?

I think people often make a huge error when setting goals: they set too many. From my own personal experience, I've found the more goals I set, the fewer I achieve. These days, when I really want to be sure that I will complete my goals, I set no more than three. Having just a few goals to work on really focuses me. It's also becomes really motivating as I make faster progress when I have fewer things on my list.

How big should your goals be? Well, they need to be grand enough to excite you, yet realistic enough that you believe you can reach them. I like Brian Tracy's rule of thumb: you should feel as though you have a 50% chance of reaching your goal.

Finally, make sure these goals are meaningful for you. Don't just choose goals because you feel it's the right thing to do. They must genuinely excite and inspire you, motivating you every day to take action. A sure sign you have the wrong goals is that the thought of working on them brings you down. Choose a goal that makes you feel good, not the people around you.

How can we handle stress with ease?

They are some wonderful techniques to reduce stress fast. I am particularly fond of *The Sedona Method* and *Transcendental Meditation*.

The Sedona Method is an incredibly simple technique of releasing your stress numerous times during the day, that way substantial stress never has a chance to build up. It was founded by a physicist named Lester Levinson, more than 30 years ago. It basically involves thinking about what's stressing you, accepting it, and then choosing to let it go.

Transcendental Meditation is an ancient but scientifically proven technique of putting yourself into an altered state that is both relaxing and invigorating. For some good research on *TM*, read Dr. Howard Benson's classic book *The Relaxation Response*. He showed that with just twenty minutes of *TM* you can reduce your stress, become more relaxed and think more creatively. Make these two techniques central in your life and you'll be calmer and more bliss-filled within a week.

How can we increase our levels of energy?

One of the fastest ways to increase your physical energy is to get passionate about your work. When you're really enthusiastic, your energy levels skyrocket.

In addition, eating smaller meals, packed with fresh fruit and vegetables, will also generate increased supplies of energy. Many fitness experts recommend eating five or six small meals a day, rather than three larger meals. That way your blood sugar levels (and therefore your energy levels) remain stable and balanced.

I've also noticed that many ambitious people don't respect sleep nearly enough. Research shows that getting seven to eight hours sleep every night improves your mood, concentration, hormone balance, creativity, memory, and of course, energy. Sleep is so much more important than most people think.

Your movement affects your energy too. For example, if you sit or walk around like you feel energetic you will indeed begin to feel that way. Move slowly with your head down and shoulders stooped and a feeling of tiredness and lethargy is virtually assured. Our body movements change our mood and vice versa.

What's the best way to manage time?

This is a fascinating area. I've been studying time management systems for over twenty years, and I'm still discovering new time saving techniques. Here are my top tips:

Rush unimportant jobs, or even better delegate them. So often we spend too much time on the unimportant. As investment genius Warren Buffett likes to say, "What's not worth doing, is not worth doing well".

Do two daily lists. The first is your list of To Do's. The second outlines what time of the day you aim to complete each of them. Many people who only do the first To Do List, discover that they have not allocated enough time to complete the list.

Do the most important task first thing in the day. This is so simple but very effective. Using this technique, you can often get several major tasks achieved by 10am.

Always have an agenda for meetings and set a time by which they will conclude.

Work with urgency; give yourself mini-deadlines to get jobs done quicker.

Constantly remind yourself of the 80/20 rule: 20 percent of what you do will give you 80 percent of your results.

If you want to research time management further I recommend *How to Get Control of Your Time and Your Life* by Alan Lakein and *Eat*

That Frog by Brian Tracy, two of the finest productivity books ever written.

How can we become more creative in life and why is it important?

Hard work doesn't guarantee success. Of course it's important, but the world is full of people working exceedingly hard and still not making it big. What is often missing is creativity and a willingness to do things like they've never been done before. That takes bravery, but such creativity is vital to get ahead of the pack.

How do you become more creative? Set aside a few minutes every day to come up with new ideas. That alone will massively boost your creativity. When you do, force yourself to come up with many ideas, rather than just one great one. The more you have, the more chance a few of them will be gems. And see yourself as being creative; imagine that you are a genius. When you expect to be creative you will become more creative. Many people do not try to be creative because they simply don't believe they have that skill. But recent research shows anyone can be highly creative if they take the time to practice being so.

Can you recommend practical ways to stimulate creativity?

I love Edward de Bono's dictionary technique. You just find a simple word from the dictionary, then try to relate it to your issue or problem. For example, if you were designing chairs and the word you chose was 'octopus', you might decide to look at creating a chair with 8 legs, like octopus tentacles. But if you chose the word 'tank', you might come up with a chair that rolls across the ground on tracks like an army tank. This technique is brilliant for coming up with unusual, highly creative ideas for just about anything.

Another useful technique is to set yourself a ten minute period where you seek to conceive an idea a minute. By really putting yourself under pressure to come up with an idea every 60 seconds, within ten minutes you will often have extraordinary creative breakthroughs.

One more technique is to pretend you're someone else. If you have a management problem, ask yourself "How would Barack Obama handle this?" If you have a people problem, ask yourself, "How would Mahatma Gandhi, Oprah Winfrey or the Pope handle it?" If it's a problem specific to your industry, ask yourself how the top person in your industry would handle it.

How can we achieve our goals when they seem insurmountable?

The answer is to just take little steps. As long as you are making progress – no matter how small – you are getting closer to your goal. It also helps to regularly remind yourself of how far you've come, rather than spend a lot of time thinking of how far you still have to go. You also need to regularly reward yourself for what you've achieved so far.

I also highly recommend modeling the actions of other people who have achieved similar things. As the saying goes, success leaves clues. Find what other people did to achieve the results you are after and do the same things. And remember the old saying "The journey is the reward". Going for the goal should be the most fun, not achieving it.

How can we increase our productivity at work?

If you ask most folks what their top three most important activities are at work, many can't immediately tell you. That lack of clarity inevitably leads to poor productivity. So get clear, really clear, about what your top three tasks are. Then make sure at least 50 percent of your day is spent doing them. If you do this, productivity will never be a problem again.

We don't really have a shortage of time. Most important activities can be done, if only we didn't spend so much time on trivial activities.

It also helps to make a list of your top three time wasters, and commit yourself to eradicating them from your life. These are very elementary techniques, but believe me, prioritizing your actions in this manner can revolutionize your effectiveness over time.

Any tips about staying upbeat and positive?

Yes. Look at how depressed people think and do the opposite! There is a structure of thinking that leads to depression. Cognitive behavior science has shown that depressed people generally (a) think their problems are more personal than they are (b) are bigger than they are, and (c) will last longer than they actually will. But if you choose to think the opposite and see problems as not being personal, huge or long lasting, your mood will lift immediately. Try it next time you're feeling down and I'm confident you'll find your mood will lighten considerably.

Other proven ways to feel upbeat are getting some sunlight every day, creating a daily gratitude list and hanging out with optimistic people. Some books I recommend on the science of happiness are *What Happy People Know* by Dan Baker and *Authentic Happiness* by Martin Seligman. And in a fascinating research study, just reading the book *Feeling Good – The New Mood Therapy* was shown to improve patients' depressed feelings, so I highly recommend that book by Dr. David D. Burns.

How can we overcome self-doubt and build confidence?

We all go through periods of doubt – even superstars in industry, sport, and the arts. However, we don't have to listen to our doubts. One of the most interesting discoveries about the mind is that it can only think one thought at a time. So that means that each time you feel unconfident, you can discipline yourself to replace that thought with another, more positive one. At first, doing this can seem hard, but stick with it and soon it will become automatic.

The day that a person decides they are going to take control of their mind, rather than let their circumstances and mood dictate their thoughts, is a great day indeed. I try to spend twenty minutes imagining my life going well each morning, as I listen to inspiring music. That way I train my mind to think positively and constructively about my future.

Why is reading a good habit to cultivate?

You can get wise in two ways. Through your own experience (slow and painful) or by learning from others (fast and easy).

But where can you find really wise people to teach you their most valuable lessons? It's certainly hard to meet them. That's where books come in. In any public library there are hundreds of books overflowing with sage advice on any subject you may be interested in learning. By simply reading their pages, you can get centuries of wisdom in just a few minutes. That's why books are so magical. Books also provide valuable perspectives, new ways of thinking, and new role models to emulate and be inspired by. I usually read between 25 and 50 books a year, almost all on personal and business development. Recent topics I've bought multiple books on include achievement, psychology, mind-body connections, spirituality, stock trading, real-estate, time management, and business excellence.

Why is it important to cultivate leadership skills in everything that we do?

We can't create great things by working alone; generally we need to enlist the help of others to produce anything significant. That's why good leadership skills are so important. Demonstrating strong leadership skills inspires others to assist you in your endeavors, thereby giving you greater success faster. When people get behind a leader, nothing is impossible. A great leader energizes, uplifts, educates, guides and gives confidence to everyone around them. That's why leaders are priceless in any family or organization.

As the great former Chief Executive of GE, Jack Welch said, the term CEO shouldn't stand for Chief Executive Officer. It should stand for Chief Energy Officer. He believed one of the CEO's most important jobs was to energize staff and make them feel empowered. This, in my opinion, is what true leadership is all about. There's only so much you can achieve yourself, no matter how dedicated or talented you are. Furthermore, trying to do it all yourself is exhausting and stressful. For a business to scale up to a massive level you need four things: a good idea; excellent systems, a team of outstanding people to make it happen and an inspired and effective leader. Without great leadership the first three will not be enough to ensure success.

Do you believe a calm, balanced life can enhance performance?

You bet I do. And so does The Human Performance Institute. Their decades of research shows that when people have family, health and spiritual goals, not just work goals, they are happier, more fulfilled and definitely more successful. That institute has also shown that leaving work at a reasonable hour, taking regular breaks and spending considerable time in recreation, recharges executives greatly. Quality recovery is critical to high performance. If your life is all work, it's almost certain you are not performing at the highest level you could be. There's nothing smart or effective about walking around exhausted all the time, yet our culture admires busyness and workaholicism. We have to resist the cultural pull to work night and day, because it's clearly been proven to be ineffective and after a while it's unsustainable.

How can we enhance our interpersonal skills and communication?

I really believe getting on with people is really simple. First, spend most of your time talking about their loves, needs, hopes and problems, not yours. Secondly, be upbeat and positive. And that's about it. Do those two things and 90 percent of people will feel warmly about you and consider you a superb communicator. Try it. Sure you can learn a mountain of clever techniques and strategies to artfully win people over, but it's unnecessary. Just follow these two simple rules and you'll be widely liked, trust me.

What is a good routine we can follow to keep a positive frame of mind?

The most important thing is to sculpt your thinking daily. Each week day I usually do visualization, pray, read an inspirational book for at least ten minutes, and talk to myself in an encouraging, inspiring way. Then in the evening I review what I did well that day and what I could have done better. I also mentally list all the things in my life that I'm grateful for, then drift off to sleep visualizing my life how I ideally want it to be.

It's a simple routine, but I think you'll find that after just a few weeks, you will feel far more inspired and positive about your life. The trick is to make it a daily system that you do habitually, rather than only go through it occasionally, so it becomes a truly powerful part of your life. But if you don't spend time each day sculpting your thinking, inevitably you will end up thinking negative, happiness-depleting thoughts. After a month or two, this destructive thinking can become habitual and over time, it becomes devastating to your peace of mind.

We must train our minds like we train our bodies. We need to give them a daily workout to keep them in top shape. This simple mental system only takes a few minutes a day, but believe me, it can be absolutely life transforming.

What are your three favorite books on personal achievement?

It's hard to go past Brian Tracy's first book, *Maximum Achievement*. It's a comprehensive analysis of the psychology of success. Brian has studied the art and science of success for more than 25 years and he really knows his stuff. There are enough strategies and techniques for high achievement within this book to keep you busy improving yourself for a decade.

Next, I have always liked *Think and Grow Rich*. First published in 1937, it is a masterpiece of the personal development genre. I read it when I was 17 and it changed my life. It's also quite a radical book (for example check out the chapter entitled "The Mystery of Sex Transmutation"). Finally *Buzan's Book of Genius* is a fascinating summary of what makes some of the world's highest achievers tick. It's written by two Mensa geniuses, Tony Buzan and Raymond Keene, a chess grandmaster. The book examines the 21 characteristics of genius then shows you practical techniques to help you become one.

There are really so many great personal achievement books that it's hard to narrow them down to just three. My bookshelf has hundreds, and almost every week I find another great one has been published. It's a beautiful thing. But of course the difficult part is not just reading great self improvement books, but putting their ideas into action.

CHAPTER 8

Enhance your thinking power for unstoppable success

Dr. Edward de Bono – International Leading Thinker

> *You cannot dig a hole in a different place by digging the same hole deeper. Lateral thinking involves the changing of approaches, concepts and perceptions rather than working harder with the existing ones.*

Biography

Edward de Bono is regarded as the global leading authority in the field of creative and conceptual thinking. An MD, PHD and Rhodes Scholar, he has authored 72 books in 41 languages. His instruction in thinking has been sought by major corporations around the world. Edward de Bono was born in Malta and graduated from the University of Malta. He proceeded as a Rhodes Scholar to Oxford, where he earned his MD, and two PhDs. He has held faculty appointments at the Universities of Oxford, Cambridge, London, and Harvard. He is the originator of the term "Lateral Thinking", which has an official entry in the *Oxford English Dictionary*, and the extremely popular "Six Thinking Hats" concept. Dr. de Bono has made the TV series: "De Bono's Thinking Course" for the BBC, and "The Greatest Thinkers" for WDR, Germany. Peter Veberroth, who organized the Olympic Games in Los Angeles, and for the first time ever turned a profit, attributed his success to the use of De Bono's Lateral thinking tools. So did John Bertrand, skipper of the successful challenge for the America's Cup. Ron Barbaro, past president of Prudential Insurance (USA) also attributed his invention of "living needs benefits" package, which revolutionized the insurance industry, to the power of the de Bono tools.

His corporate clients include: IBM, DuPont, Prudential, Siemens, Electrolux, Shell, Exxon, NTT, Motorola, Nokia, Ericsson, Ford, Microsoft, AT&T, and Saatchi, and many more. A few recent highlights include: The international Astronomical Union named a planet after Dr. de Bono in recognition of his contribution to humanity; a group of South African University professors compiled a list of the 250 most influential people in the history of humanity and included Dr. de Bono; at an International Thinking Conference in Boston, Dr. de Bono was given an award as a pioneer in the field of "teaching thinking". There are 4 million references to Dr. de Bono on the Internet.

How did you start out? What early experiences shaped the person you are today?

There is a strong tradition of medicine in my family. My father was professor of medicine. My uncle was professor of surgery and another uncle was professor of Ear, Nose and Throat. So I started out in medicine and qualified as a doctor (MD). I then proceeded as a Rhodes Scholar to Oxford where I studied psychology (MA). I returned to medicine and carried out research and teaching at the universities of Oxford, London, Cambridge, and Harvard.

In 1969 I wrote a book with the title *The Mechanism of Mind*. This book was read by the leading physicist in the world: Professor Murray Gell-Mann who was awarded the Noble Prize for discovering the quark. He liked the book very much and commissioned a team of computer experts to simulate what I had suggested in the book. They reported that it would work exactly as claimed.

So my interest in thinking came from my studies in Psychology. It seemed to me that our existing habits of thinking were excellent but not enough. Information, analysis, and logic were very good but that was only part of thinking. Instead we needed to supplement our current thinking with "lateral thinking". When I wrote my first book in 1967 *The Use of Lateral Thinking* (US title *New Think*) the sector of society that was most interest in thinking was the business sector. This has remained so to this day. I continued with medical research for many years and wrote many other books. The time came when the interest in my work grew to such an extent that I retired from medicine and devoted myself to work of the 'thinking'. This is both in the business world and also in the world of education.

It has been said that we only use a small percentage of our rain. What are the ways to enhance our brain's ability?

There are probably 100,000 people in the world writing software for the brain for 2,400 years. That is since the GG3 (Greek Gang of Three). Socrates, Plato and Aristotle developed a type of thinking and logic that we use to this day. The thinking software we use today was designed by the Greek Gang of Three (Socrates, Plato and Aristotle) 2,400 years ago. This thinking was endorsed by the Church at the time of the Renaissance and has remained as the core of our education and thinking ever since. It is 'ebne': excellent but not enough.

We developed the thinking that was 'good at finding the truth'. This has also proved very useful in science. This is the thinking taught in schools and universities. But we have never developed the thinking 'for creating value'. We are so very complacent about our traditional thinking habits and methods that we do not realize how limited and primitive they may be. In conflict situation we rush to judgment. Who is wrong? Who is at fault? We then seek to work forward from such judgments. This is because our traditional thinking is based on recognition and judgment. This is like Aristotle's boxes. Do you fall into the guilty box or outside that box? This type of thinking is common among leaders, politicians, the UN, the media etc. It is the normal and obvious reaction.

Instead of arguments we could use 'parallel thinking' and the "Six Hat Thinking". In this method, all parties look and think in the same direction at any one moment. The directions change as symbolized by the different hats. In the end a thorough and honest exploration of the subject has been achieved. You show off not by proving someone wrong but by performing better under each hat.

How can we enhance our ability to think and solve problems?

The very first step is to want to improve your thinking. If you believe you are a great thinker you will not want to take steps to improve your thinking. If you believe you are an adequate thinker you will also be complacent. If the motivation for improvement is not there you will never change your thinking. You may believe that more and more information will be enough. Information is essential and very valuable but certainly not enough. You may believe that thinking is a matter of IQ and if you do not have a high IQ there is nothing you can do. You may believe that if you do have a high IQ there is nothing you need to do. Not so, thinking and IQ are quite separate. IQ is like the horsepower and engineering of a motor car. Thinking is like the skill with which the car is driven. There are people with a high IQ who are poor thinkers. They get caught in the IQ trap.

We think in order to see if there is a better or simpler way of doing things. Adequacy can often block excellence. How do you define the problem? This is key. It is difficult to be sure you have the most useful definitions. So it is worth trying different definitions of the problem. As always, perception is important. How do you perceive the problem? How do you perceive the context of the problem? This includes the other people involved, the information available, the possible actions etc. As with all thinking, what is the objective of the thinking? It is important to be very disciplined and deliberate in your thinking. It is not enough to mess around and hope that the solution will somehow emerge. Take each step formally and deliberately.

Sometimes it might be useful to put yourself in the mind of someone else who tries to tackle the same problem. What would that other person do? What is different from the way you tackle the problem? What can you learn from this difference? Above all, watch your thinking in action. Observe what you are doing. Observe the steps you take.

What is perception and why is that sometimes more important than reality?

Perception is real even when it is not reality. We react to our perceptions of reality not to reality itself. Professor David Perkins of Harvard University showed in his research that 90 percent of the errors of thinking were errors of perception.

A very young boy was asked by his friends to choose between a one dollar coin (Australian) and a two dollar coin which is very much smaller. He was told he could keep the one he chose. He chose the large one dollar coin. His friends laughed at his stupidity. Whenever they wanted to tease him they repeated the test and he never learned but always chose the bigger coin. An adult asked him if he knew that the smaller coin was twice as valuable as the bigger one. Yes, of course, he knew that – but how often would his friends have offered him the coin if he had chosen the smaller one the first time? The perception of this boy included not only the coins themselves but his friends and their predicted behavior.

Once you have perceived something you cannot un-perceive it. Perception controls emotions and emotions control behavior. So perception is of fundamental importance to thinking – even though it has been so thoroughly neglected.

Many schools and corporations are using "Six Hat Thinking" as a way to find solutions to their problems. Can you explain what that is?

We have used argument for 2,400 years – ever since it was invented by the GG3 (Greek Gang of 3). We use it as our main method of discussion. We use it in Parliament. We use it in courts of law. We use it in family discussions.

Argument has its highest value when we seek to prove whether something did happen or did not happen – as in the courts of law. Argument can also be useful when seeking to prove or disprove a theory. In all other situations argument is primitive, crude, and inefficient. Argument is negative. Argument is about attack and defense. There is no design element. There is no attempt to reconcile different points of view. People become more concerned with their argument than with the subject itself. Argument is too much about ego and the need to feel superior by proving the other party wrong. But what could we use instead of argument? We could use 'parallel thinking'.

Imagine a building with four people each facing one side of this building. Each person, through a mobile phone, is arguing that he or she is facing the most beautiful side of the building. They could go on arguing. Instead everyone moves around to the same side: what do we all see? Then they all move around to another side. And so on until they have together looked at each side. So instead of the usual adversarial thinking where A disagrees with B there is parallel thinking. A and B are looking in the same direction. The directions, however, change.

In order to symbolize the different directions we use the symbol of the 'thinking hat' which can be put on or taken off. There are

Six Hats to symbolize six different modes of thinking. The White Hat is for information. The Red Hat is for feelings, emotions and intuition. The Black Hat is for critical thinking, caution and risk assessment. The Yellow Hat is for benefits and values. The Green Hat is for creativity, alternatives, new ideas, and modifications. The Blue Hat is for organizing the thinking: deciding the focus, deciding the sequence of Hats and putting together the outcome. There is no fixed sequence but the training course in the use of the Six Hats suggests how different sequences may be used.

What are the immediate benefits of using "Six Hat Thinking" for work and family life?

The method is now used in the boardrooms of major corporations and also by four-year-olds at school. It is used by many different cultures and nationalities around the world. The full thinking power of all those at the meeting is directed at exploring the subject – not at proving a point. The method is used widely in business where proving a point is less important than making the right decision. The method is widely used in family discussions where argument soon tends to get antagonistic. One senior executive told me that when he gets angry with his six-year-old daughter she tells him to 'take off his red hat'.

It is incredible to think that for 2,400 years we have been happy with argument. Why was something as simple and powerful as the Six Hats not invented many years ago? Probably because intellectual development was in the hands of academics who were not much concerned with practical thinking. The use of the Six Hats across different cultures and very different ages is one of its main practical advantages.

It can reduce meeting times dramatically. MDC in Canada showed that using the Hats saved them $20,000,000 in the first year alone.

Statoil in Norway had a problem with an oil rig which was costing them $100,000 a day. They had been thinking about it for two weeks. Then Jens Arup, one of my trainers, introduced the Hats and in twelve minutes they had a solution which saved them $10,000,000.

What is lateral thinking? How can we integrate that into our daily lives?

You cannot dig a hole in a different place by digging the same hole deeper. Lateral thinking involves the changing of approaches, concepts and perceptions rather than working harder with the existing ones.

We have always regarded creative thinking as a mysterious gift which some people are born with and others can only envy. For the first time in the history of humanity we can look at creative thinking as a skill which can be taught, learned, practiced, and used in a deliberate fashion. This is possible because for the first time in history we can design thinking tools based on the way the brain actually works – instead of playing around with words, which is what philosophers have had to do over the ages.

One day a fellow gets up in the morning and contemplates the eleven items of clothing he has to put on. He programs his computer to go through each of the possible ways of getting dressed with eleven items of clothing. The computer takes forty hours of processing. This is not surprising because with eleven items there are 39,916,800 ways of getting dressed. If you were to try one way every minute of your waking life you would need to live to be 76 years old – doing nothing else but trying ways of getting dressed. Life would be rather difficult. The reason we do not have to do this is that the brain allows incoming information to organize itself into patterns. Once these patterns are formed we just use the relevant pattern. That is why you can get dressed, cross the road, drive to work etc. That is why you can read and write when you get there.

We can indeed integrate the general habit of lateral thinking into our daily lives when we make an effort to change approach, change perception and change the concepts we are using. The formal tools of lateral thinking are much more powerful than the general attitude but they do need to be used in a disciplined manner.

How will lateral thinking contribute to the solution of the world's problems?

At the time of writing Israel had recently invaded Gaza in order to stop the rockets which had been fired at Israel over many years. In the course of the invasion many people were killed and much damage was done. The rockets still continued. The response of the Israeli government to the rocket bombardment was traditional. You stop force with more force. Here is a more lateral solution. The nations that set up Israel should together set up an annual donation to the Palestinians of about three billion dollars. But every time a rocket is fired at Israel the Palestinians lose fifty million dollars. So those firing the rockets are no longer heroes but very expensive and have a cost a school or a hospital etc.

In Zimbabwe, President Mugabe is reluctant to relinquish power after 28 years as leader of the nation. As a result other nations withhold the economic support which is so badly needed. Eventually a power-sharing agreement is reached. A lateral solution would be to give Mugabe the permanent title of 'Father of the Nation', which he deserves. He gets a palace and an income. He also has the right to veto any three bills a year in parliament. All these are for his lifetime. He might then be willing to step aside from politics. To ask him simply to disappear after 20 years as leader is not so acceptable.

Lateral solutions are not necessarily the best or the only solution. They are additional and alternative approaches. Such solutions may be used directly or they may suggest other approaches. The important thing is that they move away from the traditional approach. You cannot dig a hole in a different place by digging the same hole deeper. Our traditional habits of thinking insist that you must attack an idea and prove it to be wrong before you start looking for a better idea. With lateral thinking you acknowledge the value of the existing idea but still set out to look for a better idea.

You say that the major problem facing the earth and humanity is the inadequacy of our thinking. Please explain and elaborate.

The Greek Gang of three left us with mental software which depends very much on judgment. We are always making judgments about the nature of something: good person, bad person, hero, traitor etc.

Two thousand years ago China was ahead of Europe in terms of science and technology. They had gunpowder and rockets among other things. Had China continued along this growth path, today China would probably be the dominant power in the world in science, technology, economics etc. What happened? What went wrong?

It seems that the scholars became very arrogant. They believed that it was enough to examine the facts and the evidence and to draw logical conclusions. They were not interested in speculation, imagination and possibilities. So progress came to a dead end. They were interested in 'what is' and lost interest in 'what can be'. I once tried to set up at the UN a creative group to provide alternative ways forward and possibilities in crisis situations. This quickly proved impossible. I was told that people were there to represent their countries and not to think.

So we need to supplement our habits of argument and judgment with parallel thinking (Six Hats) and design. The real problem is our huge complacency with our existing thinking habits. We really do believe they are excellent. This is partly because of our success in science and technology and partly because we only judge our thinking with the idioms of that very same thinking. Most people would rate climate change as the biggest problem facing humanity. I disagree. I believe the inadequacy of our thinking software is the real fundamental problem. If we improve that we would be able to deal even more effectively with climate change.

To solve a problem, why is it that sometimes experience, information, analysis, and logic are not enough?

Experience will help us apply routines from the past. Experience will allow us to apply the standard responses that have worked before. Experience allows us to recognize situations. George Santayana has a very well known saying: "If you do not learn from the mistakes of the past you are condemned to repeat them." This is certainly both true and valuable. But there is another quotation (my own). "If you learn too well from the successes of the past you are doomed to be trapped by them."

This means that we tend to apply the same thinking and the same solutions if they have worked before. This effectively blocks us from doing any new thinking. The adequate may well block the best. Because we have an adequate way of doing something we make no further thinking effort. In such cases experience is as much negative as it is positive.

Information, analysis and logic are enough. This, unfortunately, is the general belief of most thinkers today. Because, hitherto, we had no means of using creative thinking in a deliberate and formal manner, so this type of thinking had to be left out. Today with lateral thinking an element of creative thinking can be used at every stage in thinking.

Our traditional thinking methods are in no way incorrect – but they are incomplete. We need to add these newer aspects of thinking to our existing methods (perceptual, creative, design, parallel etc.).

How can we enhance our communication skills on every level?

Some time ago the US Joint Chiefs of Staff banned the use of PowerPoint at their meetings. This is because that system allows someone seeking to communicate, to create long lists of points projected from a computer. This may "express" the view of the communicator but is not much use to the viewer who has to sort through all this information.

This first step towards improving communication is to shift attention from the communicator to those who are to receive the communication. Too many communications are ego-exercises on the part of the communicator and incomprehensible to the listener or viewer.

In good communication there is a need to have a great deal of sensitivity about the receiver. What concepts does the receiver use? What values matter to the receiver? What are the existing perceptions and how can they be changed? Too much communication is like firing a shotgun into the air and hoping it hits some passing bird. Simplicity is essential in communication – as in many other areas. Wherever possible, communications should be made interesting.

What is your vision of an ideal world?

It would be possible to suggest all sorts of improved structures. There are many possible improvements toward a better world. Rather than all those possibilities I shall narrow it down to three basic habits and skills, which everyone should learn, practice and develop.

    a)   The first such habit is "Happiness". I once wrote a book with the title *The Happiness Purpose*. This was all about being happy. There may be many different approaches to this matter. The important point is that we need to develop happiness as a habit.
Happiness is not just the absence of illness, misery, tragedy, problems etc. Happiness is not just the white on the white of the canvas when there are no other marks on that area.
Happiness is something definite and deliberate in its own right.
It is not just the gaps between unhappiness. From an early age youngsters must be encouraged to be happy. This is not just a matter of more toys and sweets. Happiness is a yellow splash on the canvas, not just the absence of other marks.

    b)   The next habit is being "Positive". This does overlap with happiness but is different. Being positive usually leads to happiness – and the other way around. It is, however, possible to be positive even when you are not happy. Being positive is possibly an easier habit to learn than being happy. There is nothing that is improved by being gloomy, depressed, annegative. You make an effort to find positive aspects in things even if this is sometimes rather hard.

Being positive means being positive in reaction to events we cannot control. Being positive means setting out to do things that are positive in nature. Being positive means helping others to be positive and leading them to be positive. Being negative feeds upon itself and encourages everyone around to be negative. Negativity is too often a form of self-indulgence where the world and others can be blamed when things are not exactly as you would like them. Being positive breaks the vicious cycle of negativity. Being positive does not mean resignation and acceptance of whatever fate throws up. It is possible to be positive and to be very active.

    c)   The third habit is "thinking". Many educated people claim that they think this is often not the case. Such people analyze the situation to identify a standard element and then they apply the standard solution. This often works well enough – but that is only a poor form of thinking. From an early age youngsters would be taught the full habits of perceptual thinking. They would learn the parallel thinking of the Six Hats which they can use as an alternative to adversarial argument. They would learn the formal tools of lateral thinking so they could set out to be creative in a deliberate way instead of just sitting and waiting for ideas.

With these three habits in place human beings can set out to improve the world and to construct better institutions and frameworks. Conflicts and disputes would not arise. If they arouse they can be settled by designed rather than by judgment.

Albert Einstein said that "The significant problems we face cannot be solved at the same level of thinking we were at when we created them." How do you think his statement is relevant to today's world?

Einstein was a natural lateral thinker. He was always challenging accepted beliefs.

His quotation is very relevant to today's problems. In most cases the thinking that created the problem was judgment thinking. That meant putting people and issues into labeled boxes and keeping them there. You then treated the situation according to the label on the box. Einstein may have meant that the problems were created in the first place by our limited thinking. This is indeed often the case. It is also the case that however the problem was created in the first place it will not adequately be solved by our limited thinking.

Just to condemn our traditional thinking as limited is not enough. It is important to suggest alternatives and improvements. For examples was can shift the emphasis from judgment to design. We can seek to use the creativity of lateral thinking. We can use parallel thinking instead of argument. All these suggestions are practical and do-able. Even the shift from judgment to design on its own will have a powerful effect.

Why is problem solving such a big problem in thinking?

Many people, especially in North America, regard the purpose of thinking to be 'problem solving'. They probably mean that any thinking task you set yourself becomes a problem to be tackled. The general effect, however, of treating thinking as 'problem-solving' is that we only apply our thinking to perceived problems.

The Bill and Melinda Gates Foundation give generously to the treatment of AIDS in Africa. There are other problems which are helped by the generosity of the foundation. Other foundations behave in a similar manner. There are obvious problems to be solved. Suppose I were to ask one of these foundations for help in 'improving human thinking', what would happen. I have tried, so I know. The foundations make it clear that they are only in the problem-solving business.

There is a great deal of thinking that needs to be done – but it is not problem-solving. You can say that 'the improvement of human thinking is the problem that I want to solve'. Nevertheless, that project will not get funding because it is not perceived as a visible problem – no matter how much I may consider it to be a very important problem. This is a bit like medicine only being concerned with defined illnesses and not paying attention to general health and well-being. Most aspects of life need periodic thinking attention whether there are defined problems or not. They need to get that attention for dedicated thinking groups – perhaps working under the direction of the new Ministry for Thinking.

Thinking is not just about problem solving. There is a need to think about everything and anything.

How can we create a better world?

The simple and direct answer is to teach thinking at all levels in education from primary school to university. Research already shows that teaching thinking reduces violent crime by 90 percent; increases employment by 500 percent; and improves performance in every subject by between 30 and 100 percent. Society needs those changes. We need to move away from our judgment and logic type thinking to thinking that uses design and creativity.

We may need to introduce parallel thinking (Six Hats) instead of parliamentary argument. The emphasis on design would be applied to large business and to small business. The financial system would need to be designed to make impossible the recent dangerous excesses. The media might be encouraged to be more positive in their outlook even if this is far more difficult than being negative. Maybe every newspaper should have one positive page in each issue. Universities would no longer just teach knowledge, which can be obtained elsewhere in the digital world. Universities would teach skills: information skills;

thinking skills; people skills; management skills; entrepreneurial skills; ecology skills etc. Universities would have a faculty of 'thinking'.

Happiness and positive attitudes would be encouraged and even trained. Complaints and grumbling would be regarded as sometimes necessary but a low-level contribution to society. There would be awards for new ideas that improved or simplified society. Thinking would be treated as being of equal importance to rugby or cricket.

Many people would like to make a difference in the world. Where can they begin?

Learning to think enables a person to take control over his or her life. So teaching someone to think is likely to have more effect than anything else on individuals and on the world in general. Learning thinking reduces crime dramatically, increases employment hugely and has a powerful effect on business performance.

So if you want to make a difference in the world, one sure way is to encourage and promote the direct teaching of thinking as a skill. This may be done through inclusion in the school curriculum. Thinking may be included in foundation courses in universities. You may set out to teach thinking to under-privileged groups. You may encourage developing countries to pay more attention to this important subject.

Is there something we could do today to make immediate changes to our lives?

I could suggest that people read my books. Now it could be that these people learned something from books. It could also be that my books re-assured them that their own natural thinking was indeed valid –

even when school had told them otherwise. There are many examples of people who have told me that reading one of my books changed their lives. There is Ashok Chouhan who bought my first book at a bookstore at Paris airport and kept it in his briefcase for 30 years. He told me that at that time he had three dollars in the pocket. Today he has three billion dollars in his pocket and that was 80 percent due to reading my book. At a seminar in Barcelona a man came up to me and told me that at school he was useless. Then he read one of my books and now he owns seven different businesses in Spain. There are many, many others.

It is also important to realize that thinking is not only for problem solving. We can also think about things which are not problems and seem perfectly satisfactory. Thinking about such things may suggest an improvement or even a whole new way of doing things. It may be useful to set aside some formal time each day for just sitting and thinking. You can set up a focus list and then work steadily through it. The discipline involves sitting there and just thinking about the focus and noting down some of the thoughts. A family could set aside one evening a week where the whole family had a thinking session. This would be both fun and educational. The thinking tools would be learned and used both on real life situations and also fictional ones. Another step would be to learn the Six Hats method and to use it both in the family and at work instead of argument in discussion sessions. The same applies to the lateral thinking tools.

CHAPTER 9

Unleashing your heart's desire

Sonia Choquette – Professional Life Coach

> *Intuition originates in our hearts and then resonates throughout our body, using our other senses at times to guide and lead us – beyond our conscious intellectual mind – to make the best possible decisions for ourselves on a moment to moment basis.*

Biography

Sonia Choquette is a unique and extraordinary spiritual teacher, intuitive guide and masterful catalyst. She is the best-selling author of ten books published in more than 30 countries: *The Psychic Pathway, Your Heart's Desire, The Intuitive Spark, True Balance, The Diary of a Psychic, Trust Your Vibes, Ask Your Guides, Soul Lessons and Soul Purpose,* **and** *The Time Has Come.* She has also produced numerous lively audio editions and meditations. Sonia has been a personal intuitive adviser to such New Age Leaders as Louise Hay, Julia Cameron, Caroline Myss, Dr. Wayne Dyer, and pop icon Billy Corgan of the Smashing Pumpkins rock band. She also serves as a professional consultant to international business CEOs of companies such as Charlotte Beers, and Fortune 500 Company.

Sonia is passionate, dynamic, powerful, and direct in her ability to instantly liberate people from their limitations and fears (a five-sensory life) and leads them to create a far more effective, spirit guided (six sensory) successful life, which she insists is "our natural way". Using her highly developed, finely tuned intuitive skills she can instantly identify self sabotaging patterns and life obstacles and guide people past them to achieve success in all their goals. No-nonsense, to-the point, practical, down-to-earth, and often hilarious in her delivery, Sonia's intuitive gifts and engaging spirit inspire even the most cynical. There is no doubt about it; to meet Sonia in person is to change your life.

Her book *Your Heart's Desire* is currently required reading at the University of Santa Monica and her book *The Wise Child* was a featured topic at the first International Conference on Children's Spirituality in Atlanta, sponsored by the University of Atlanta. Sonia has been a regular guest on ABC, NBC, CNN, FOX, Lime, Sirius, and WGN as well as featured in *New Woman Magazine* (where they rated *Your Heart's Desire* as one of the ten best books to change your life), *New Age Magazine, USA Today, Body and Soul, Chicago Tribune, Chicago Sun Times* and *Crain's Chicago Business Journal*.

Highly trained and apprenticed in both the Psychic Arts and Metaphysical Law, Sonia was educated at the University of Denver and the Sorbonne in Paris. She then pursued a spiritual education at the American Institute of Holistic Theology resulting in a BA, MS and PhD in Metaphysics. However, she insists that her best education is the result of over 35 years of working "in the trenches," consulting directly with people, and conducting one-on-one readings all over the world. Sonia resides in Chicago with her husband, her two daughters and their poodle, Miss T.

How did you start out? What early experiences shaped the person you are today?

Whenever I am asked how I started my work as an intuitive guide and spiritual teacher, I have to pause because I do not ever remember a specific time when I actually started on this path. It seems as though it was always my path, my way to listen to the heart, to use my inner guidance for myself and others, and encourage others to do the same. I was raised in what I call a six-sensory family, where intuition was a natural and necessary guidepost to all our family discussions and decisions. Following my mother's lead, I was taught, along with my siblings, from the earliest age that I had an inner voice, located in my heart, that served as a direct lifeline to source or divine consciousness. If I ever needed to make a decision, find an answer or needed direction, this is where I could turn for reliable guidance. This was the way my mother lived and the way she raised me. Following the intuitive heart was natural and it worked.

What do you believe is the best way for a person to find their purpose in life?

The best way for a person to find their purpose in life is to notice what they love; what they lose themselves in, what excites and delights them, and never fails to satisfy their spirit, and do that. Our purpose in life is to be happy and enjoy the process of fulfillment. Once this discovery is made, they should focus on doing what brings them joy. Purpose, however, is not necessarily profession, and many people mix this up. Our purpose is our contribution to life, and I believe that the greatest contribution we can make is to be happily engaged in what we love.

What do you believe to be the secret to true happiness?

The secret of true happiness is two-fold; first we must learn to differentiate between our ego and our Spirit. The way to do this is simple. Our ego self-selects out of life and views the world as something out there to be feared and defended against. The Spirit on the other hand, self- selects into life, viewing others as kindred spirits, recognizing that we are all unique but intimately connected expressions of this same Spirit, and engages in and enjoys life. We must tame the ego – which is always miserable, threatened, and insecure – and cultivate our spirit, which is always spontaneous, open, and receptive to the goodness of life. Secondly, we must dedicate ourselves to be in service to others in whatever way we feel we can best contribute. We experience true happiness when we make our interest in bettering the whole more important than simply satisfying our own immediate needs.

How would you define genuine greatness?

Genuine success is the ability to feel good in your own skin. It is the ability to live creatively, make choices that reflect love and authentic intention, be open and generous with everyone you encounter, and go to sleep at night with peace in your heart and loved ones in your life.

What is the difference between desires of the heart and desires of the mind?

Heart's desires reflect your most authentic self. They are desires that expand your ability to express your gifts so you can serve the betterment of the world while creating joy in your own life. Desires of the mind, on the other hand, often reflect the opinions of others, are based on a need for approval, and are rooted in fear and a desire to control life. Heart's desires come from your most authentic self and when fulfilled leave you deeply satisfied and peaceful, while mental desires come from an insecure ego, and leave you restless, unfulfilled and empty.

How can we find out what our heart's true desire is? Why is this important?

To find your true heart's desire, simply put your hand on your heart and fill in the following statement; "If I weren't afraid I would ..." Do this out loud for three full minutes, and then consider what your heart revealed. True heart's desires lie just behind fear. Ask fear to step aside in this way and your deepest heart's desires will be instantly revealed.

What are the most important principles to adhere to in the manifestation of our desires and dreams?

There are nine basic principles to creating your heart's desire. Each principle builds on the one before, creating a spiral of energy that once in process pulls in life force from the Universe to manifest your intentions. These principles are:

    Focus on Your Dream

    Gain the Support of Your Subconscious Mind

    Imagine Your Dream

    Eliminate Your Obstacles

    Be Open to Guidance

    Choose to Support Your Dream with Love

    Surrender Control

    Claim Your Dream

    Be True To Your Dream

What is the subconscious mind? How can we make it work for us at a practical level?

Our subconscious mind is our conscious mind's greatest ally. It is the part of our consciousness that puts our creative energy into flow. Like a deputy, the subconscious mind obediently follows the orders of the conscious mind. It is virtually a "Yes" machine that agrees with our conscious minds and then sets about making our conscious flow of thoughts a reality. The best way to influence the subconscious mind is through repetition. The more we repeat something, the more deeply our subconscious mind accepts and executes its orders.

How do we reprogram our subconscious mind?

The best way to reprogram the subconscious mind is to speak to it in simple, direct statements, focused in present time. The results will amaze you. For example, say, out loud, "I am happily employed," versus "I want a new job." "I am in love with the perfect for me partner;" instead of "I want love in my life." Another way to easily reprogram the subconscious mind and have fun at the same time is to make up a simple rhyme that suggests your heart's desire and sing it over and over. For example, "I am in love with life. I am in love with me. I have all that I need. I accept gleefully." I just made that up. It's catchy, easy to remember and makes me smile. And I can sing it all day long. The subconscious mind will internalize the message of the song and set about to make it so.

How do our beliefs affect our life's outcomes? How can we find out what our beliefs are?

Our beliefs are the fuel of our creative expression. What we believe becomes true. For example, two people can go into downtown Chicago on Friday afternoon and look for a free parking space. One believes he will find one, while the other believes he won't. They will both be right, although one won't be paying for a spot. See what I mean? To find out what your beliefs are, all you have to do is observe your life. It is an accurate and honest mirror of your beliefs. For example, a couple I know is married but do not share the same beliefs about life. The woman believes life is good, that she is blessed and that the Universe will take care of her no matter what. Her husband, on the other hand, believes that life is dangerous, that he can trust no one fully, and that at any moment chaos could ruin his life. She just got a promotion in her job, while he got laid off. She won tickets to San Francisco in a drawing at the bank, while he lost his wallet and all his cash. She just inherited a car from a friend who was moving to New York while he just got ripped off at the local car repair shop for new brakes that didn't work. They are both tremendously effective creators. They just believe different things.

How can we eliminate negative beliefs to achieve our heart's desire?

Often we don't believe that what we want to create is possible and that is why we don't manifest it. But we can overcome our doubt by surrounding ourselves with what I call Believing Eyes. In other words, find people who believe in your dreams and ask them to encourage you in the moments when you feel overcome by doubt. For example, many years ago, my heart's desire was to write a book and yet I doubted my ability to do so. My good friend, Julia Cameron, knew of my desire and unwaveringly encouraged me to write for six months, telling me all the while what a good book it would be. I was filled with doubt, but I nevertheless, I trusted her belief in me until I started to feel a belief in myself. With her support I continued to write through all my doubt and fear and the result was my very first book, *The Psychic Pathway*, completed six months later and published a year after that. It was a psychic collaboration between my dream and her support, and without her "Believing Eyes" I doubt I would have stayed the course and succeeded.

What is the difference between desiring an outcome and intending an outcome?

While desire is the spark and catalyst for creativity, intention is the staying power of creativity. Intention is royal desire. Intention transforms desire from mere wishful thinking to committed action. Once intention is truly engaged, nothing will get in the way.

When facing challenges and obstacles, why is it important to remain graceful, balanced and grateful?

Overcoming obstacles is the sport of creating your heart's desire. If you get intimidated by obstacles you lose your focus, intention, and imagination for success. Remaining graceful, balanced and grateful will strengthen your immunity to the infection of fear and doubt, and will keep you connected to divine flow throughout the process of manifesting what you want. Gratitude especially reminds you that no matter what obstacle is facing you, at any given moment, it will give way, just as it always has in the past. Or if not, you will be shown another way to proceed. The best way to remain centered when challenged is to breathe through your obstacles and see them melting before your eyes, like magic. If you do this, they will.

In the process of achieving, why is it important to surrender and let go?

While we are creative beings, we must also remember that we are co-creators with the Universe and that ultimately, the Universe is in charge. I suggest we tell the Universe what we desire, but let the

Universe show us how that intention will unfold. If we insist on controlling the process, we will draw only from the resources we already know – which are limited – and not from the unknown, where all things are possible. That is why it is important to surrender to the Universe's plan once we do our part in creating our heart's desire. Remember, while we can select the seed of our intention, prepare the ground, plant the seed and water it with our love and attention, we are not the ones that cause the seed to grow. We can only create the perfect conditions and, when we do, we have to trust that the Universe will grow the seeds for us. Once we do our part, we must then surrender control and allow the Universe to work on our behalf.

Most people cannot practice detachment because it feels like letting go of control. What do you have to say about this?

To detach is to realize that while our egos feel as though they are in control, they never really are. The Universe is in control – and thank goodness it is. I suggest practicing detachment by holding something, such as a small rubber stress ball, tightly in your hand, and then simply opening up your fingers, release it, and let it drop. If we can train the physical body to detach, the mind will follow its lead. To detach doesn't mean to give up. It means to step back and allow. Imagine detaching as trying to push and push and push on a door only to have it remain stuck, and then stepping back, and letting go, realizing it opens inward.

Most people want guarantees before they are willing to take a step forward. How can we learn to let go and develop faith?

Creativity requires commitment. If you want to manifest something new, you must commit to making it happen. Without commitment there can be no creative outcome. If you hold a packet of seeds in your hand and refuse to plant them until you are guaranteed they will grow, you will never enjoy the fruits of the seeds. This is because the guarantee doesn't come from the outside realm. The guarantee of success comes from within, from your intention and willingness to stick with the creative process until the end. You are the one that decides the outcome of your intentions by the investment of your own efforts. One of the best ways to overcome fear of disappointment is to work with faith. My favorite definition of faith is "confidence in the future based on what you are doing in the present". In other words, thoroughly do your part, step-by-step by following the nine principles of manifestation, and your dreams will come about naturally. Don't cheat. Don't skip steps. Don't be impatient. And do recognize your past successes. This will give you the faith to stay the course.

What is visualization? Does visualizing our goal quicken the process of manifestation?

Visualization is a very important tool in the creative process. It is the practice of engaging our inner mental screen and though our imagination seeing our creation as already fulfilled in our mind's eye. The power of visualization cannot be overstated. Simply look around your surroundings at this very moment. Everything you see was first envisioned or visualized in someone's mind before it came into the physical form. We cannot create what we cannot visualize. And yet, we always create what we do clearly visualize. Visualization breathes vitality into your heart's desire and brings it to life.

Can you recommend a practical exercise to stimulate creative visualization?

A practical way to stimulate visualization is to find actual examples of what you want to manifest. For example, if you want to manifest a great job, look around your world – on television, in magazines, or in the world around you – for what you consider good jobs and then study their details. The same goes for manifesting a great relationship. Find examples of great relationships, ones that possess the qualities that you want to experience. This process works in every aspect of life, from the most lofty to the most mundane. For example, when she was fourteen years old, my daughter desperately wanted a Chanel purse. Every day for a year, she would visualize herself with a Chanel purse, looking in fashion magazines for inspiration. I, on the other hand, could definitely not see a Chanel purse in her hand, at least one that was purchased by me. Recognizing me as not belonging to her team of "Believing Eyes", she shared her vision with others instead. At the end of the year, an elderly person whom she had helped from time to time surprised her with a genuine Chanel purse for Christmas, just as she had visualized. This is a classic illustration of the power and magic of visualization combined with faith. It happened. She got what she wanted from a source she could never have predicted in advance, just by visualizing it on a consistent basis.

What is intuition? Why do you say that it is natural and important part of us?

Intuition literally means inner teacher, which is exactly what our intuition is. It is the voice of our spirit, our Higher Self, the most informed aspect of our being. Intuition originates in our hearts and then resonates throughout our body, using our other senses at times to guide and lead us – beyond our conscious intellectual mind – to make the best possible decisions for ourselves on a moment to moment basis. Intuition manifests in a number of ways and each individual experiences it in their own personal way. Some, for example, may experience intuition as a gut feeling, while others connect with their intuition by getting chills up their spine, or feeling hairs rising on the back of the neck, or an inner voice or a feeling in their chest or throat area. No matter how intuition gets your attention, it is always conveyed by some sort of subtle energetic vibration rippling through your body and awareness. This key word here is subtle, so subtle in fact that it can go unnoticed if one is not paying attention. Intuition is our natural guidance system, our inner barometer, our own GPS system, if you will. Just as all things in nature are guided, so too are we. Birds and butterflies have their own radar that can take them from North America to South America; whales have sonar that leads them successfully across oceans. We humans have intuition, or as I like to call it, "Vibes". The reason it is so important to our lives is that it is the natural feedback and communication system that protects, guides, and keeps us in alignment with our most authentic selves. Without intuition, we get hopelessly lost in the confusion of the world and come to doubt who we are and even the purpose of life itself. Intuition reminds us what is true and genuine for our personal souls and keeps us safe, sound, and true to ourselves.

Is there any scientific proof that intuition works?

Science is slowly getting on board in recognizing intuition as a fully viable, natural part of our biological makeup. Right now, in fact, there is a report on WebMD that cites the actual physical location of the brain where intuitive messages are fired. Be patient with science. It will soon catch up with what the Spirit knows. I believe intuition is not only natural but is also necessary to help us live up to our fullest potential.

Do you believe in synchronicity and that everything happens for a reason?

I believe that we are all energetically and spiritually interconnected with one another, with Higher Spiritual forces, and with our source, or God, at all times. We experience this interconnection through synchronicity, which occurs when the hidden connection between all things gets activated and comes into play in our lives. Therefore, everything does happen for a reason, and if we are aware of this connection, the synchronicities in our lives accelerate, thereby fully supporting our intentions and rendering our lives even magical.

Is intuition an inborn talent, or can anyone develop it?

Intuition is the voice of our Spirit, and therefore it is an inborn faculty. We all have intuitive ability, but the degree to which it is developed is different in all people. Those who value and recognize intuition as important sharpen their intuitive skills rather quickly, while those who are ill-informed and ignore their intuition can effectively tune it out. Fortunately, because our intuition – or sixth sense – is an inborn and natural faculty, anyone can awaken and develop it to a very higher degree with attention, meditation, and practice.

How can we enhance our intuitive abilities?

I suggest a four-step method to best enhance our intuitive abilities.

Step One is to be open to your intuition. Imagine that your intuition is like a radio station broadcasting important news across the airwaves. Being open to intuition is like turning your personal radio receiver to the ON position in order to receive the news. People who are open to intuition are much more intuitive than those who aren't.

Step Two is to expect your intuition to work. Expectation creates a void or a vacuum that demands to be filled. Those who expect to be intuitive are. Those who expect NOT to be intuitive aren't. Going back to the analogy of the radio, being OPEN is turning the intuitive radio receiver on, and expected to be guided is like tuning directly into the radio broadcast of your Higher Self.

Step Three is to trust your intuition when it does arise. When it comes to intuition, most people have very sharp intuitive hindsight or what I call a keen sense of "woulda, coulda, shoulda". They feel guided, yet they choose to ignore it, only to regret it later. The best way to overcome this habit and start to trust your intuition, or "vibes" is to get a small pocket notebook or tape recorder, and every time you get a gut feeling, a hunch, a heightened sense of awareness, or any other inkling of an intuitive sense, write it down in your notebook or record it on your voice recorder. Do this for two weeks. What you will discover while doing this is that the more you acknowledge your intuition, the stronger and more frequent it appears. Also, in two short weeks you will have evidence in your notebook that it is real and can be trusted. Having said this, however, I know many people won't go to the trouble of recording their intuitive feelings. So I have a Plan B. I call this the "If You Name IT, You Claim IT" plan. Again, it is important to openly acknowledge your intuitive feelings every time they come up, but instead of writing them down, or recording them on a voice recorder, simply speak them out. Just say out loud, "My intuition is telling me..." and then fill in the blank every time you feel an intuitive impulse. Do not concern yourself with whether or not it is accurate or even intuitive. Simply announce out loud all vibes as they occur. You don't have to announce it to anyone in particular. Just announce it to yourself. This works almost as well as my first suggestion, but it isn't as dramatic or as fun as re-visiting your written or recorded intuitive feeling later and having them validated along the way.

Step Four is perhaps the most important of the four decisions and the one that will change your life and put intuition to work for you, and that is to ACT on your intuition when it does present itself. Start by inviting your intuitive muscles to work. Play fun games with it – "psychic sit-ups", as I like to call them. When the phone rings, check your vibes to see who it is before checking caller ID. When traveling to work, ask your vibes which is the best route to take to miss out on the traffic. When speaking to someone ask your vibes to indicate what they really mean. And LISTEN, only with your heart and not with your intellect.

In summary, have a open attitude, expect intuition to show up because it is natural, trust what you sense in your heart, and follow through on your intuition with your decisions. Play games with your intuition, and avoid trying to be "right". Simply ask yourself what feels true for you, and answer out loud as opposed to thinking the answer. Soon you will sense your intuition kicking into gear in your life.

And finally, have fun with discovering your intuition. Being intuitive is an art – a function of the creative right brain – not a science or an analytic process arising from the left brain.

Please give us an example of how we can use our intuition practically in our daily life.

Intuition is a practical faculty to develop because it can save you time, prevent mistakes, assist you in making the best decisions, offer guidance on your health, keep you in tune with significant others, and connect you with all you need to succeed in life. And best of all, it makes life more fun and exciting and delivers lots of gifts.

For example, a client recently told me that she had a strong intuition from out of nowhere to call an old artist friend from college. Because she had not seen him for fourteen years, her hunch seemed odd, but she followed through anyway. She hunted him down only to discover that he had just recently moved from the small town where they attended high school together to the same city – and even same neighborhood – where she was now living. That alone was a synchronistic surprise, but even better was the fact that he lived with his brother, whom once she met she ended up marrying. Had she not followed through on her hunch, or if she had over analyzed it into submission, she may never have met the love of her life.

This fun example aside, intuition can save you time by guiding you to more quickly find what you are looking for, whether it's your car keys, a new job, or even your purpose in life. It can warn against dangers and alert you to important details that will help you make better decisions. This past year, my intuition warned me to move all my retirement investments and put them into cash. Two months later, the bank systems and mortgage systems in American collapsed, creating the greatest stock market drop since the Great Depression. My money, on the other hand, was safe, and unchanged, which could not be said for most investors in our country at the time.

Another practical way in which intuition can help you is when assessing people. Several years ago I advertised online for an assistant and received almost 3000 job responses to the ad. My intuition told me to pick only one from the huge pile of applications and so I did. It turns out the one and only response I followed up on and subsequently hired was trained as a teenager by a dear and trusted work colleague of mine ten years earlier. Not only was he well suited for the job, he had the finest work ethic of anyone I had ever met. Seven years later we are now business partners. I thank my intuition for this stroke of good fortune.

What is meditation? What are its benefits, and how do we get started?

Meditation is simply learning to quiet our mental chatter and tune into a deeper level of spiritual awareness that lies behind our endless mind noise. The benefits of meditation cannot be overstated. It calms the nervous system, clears our thinking, relieves stress and anxiety sharpens our creativity, tunes us into our Higher Self and enhances our intuitive faculties. Learning to meditate starts with a simple decision to do it. It is far more a skill of determination that one of complexity.

Meditation begins with the breath. To start, breathe in slowly to the count of four, hold your breath to the count of four, and then slowly exhale to the count of four. Do this ten times, and then allow yourself to relax into a more relaxed and comfortable breathing pattern. Next, every time you inhale, say to yourself the words, "I am…" and when you exhale say the word, "Calm." Continue breathing in to the words "I am…" and out to the word "calm" for 10 to 20 minutes. Feel calm. Think calm. Envision calm as you do this. If your mind wanders, simply go back to the breath and start again. Remain calm and relaxed as you breathe. Remember, you are training your mind to surrender to your breath and it may take a few tries before the mind gets the idea. Stay with it and don't give up. Soon your mind will cooperate. After a few tries the mind will look forward to the mental rest and surrender more quickly into calm, peaceful, relaxed quiet. This is all it takes to meditate.

Does meditation enhance our intuitive abilities? Please share with us some practical exercises?

Among other things, one excellent benefit of meditation is that it greatly enhances our intuition. When we learn to quiet our mental chatter, we begin to tune into the deeper, calmer, quieter voice of our spirit. This deeper voice is not audible, but rather a warm, comforting vibration that resonates deep within our hearts. We cannot sense this more subtle intuition vibration if our minds are jumping up and down with anxious thoughts, judgments, and endless commentary on the world. It is only when we quiet the chatter of the mind that we can tune in to the deeper expression of the soul.

To rejuvenate our body and mind, why is it important to allocate time to plan and do nothing?

In addition to meditation, taking a few minutes in the day to relax and do nothing is another great way to both rejuvenate and refine our intuitive abilities. Allowing the mind to daydream, float, relax, rest, and "chill," as my children would say, opens the portals to higher awareness and allows more inspired thoughts to enter into our stream of consciousness. But if we are too busy and our lives are filled up with too much activity and commotion, intuition will not be able to enter our awareness as it has too many external factors competing with it.

You don't need to have a lot of free daydreaming time to gain its benefits. A ten minute siesta – maybe just looking out the window while enjoying a cup of tea – can give access to our intuitive channels. Many of my own intuitive hits came through doing just that. Relaxed daydreaming is also a wonderful activity to engage in when your creativity is blocked.

Simply stare out the window or into space and dreamily close your eyes and breathe in deeply for several minutes and relax. Just watch the world go by. This not only relieves stress, it also rejuvenates the creative mind and allows it to speak over our ego mind. Intuition is subtle and cannot compete with our mental chatter. One has to quiet the mind to hear the Spirit.

What is the best advice you have ever received?

The best advice I ever received was from my mother when I was around eight years old. She said, "Sonia, you have an inner direct lifeline to heaven and it lies in the center of your heart. Whenever you need help, guidance, or don't know which way to go or what to do, simply put your hand over your heart and breathe. This activates your connection to God. Then ask your heart what to do. It will answer through you. Just say, 'My heart says…' and see what comes through. That is the answer for you and it can always be trusted. You know your heart is reliable because you will feel a satisfied and peaceful vibration deep within when you let it guide you. Always trust this. Always trust your vibes." To this day, I do.

Do you have a ritual that you perform on a daily basis to keep yourself positive and strong?

I keep positive and strong by starting every day with this simple prayer before I even get out of bed:

Holy Spirit Divine

Mother Father God

Use me this day Move through me

Move my thoughts Move my actions

Move my heart and words

Move everything in me to serve you

Use me to bring love, light and laughter to the world this day

I am grateful to serve Your light

Amen

At the end of the day I send with this simple prayer :

Holy Spirit

Divine Mother Father God

Thank you for the gift of this day

Please forgive all errors and mistakes I have made

As I forgive all errors and mistakes made toward me

Please amplify and grow all goodness I set in motion this day

Heal all discordant thoughts, emotions, and energies in my body in the night while I sleep

And allow me to awake rested and ready to serve another day tomorrow

Amen

Many people would like to make a difference in the world. Where can they begin?

Many years ago, my spiritual teacher taught me that the best way to help the miserable world is to not be miserable myself. I thought this was very sound advice. The best way I know to contribute to this world is to be happy. And as far as I know this occurs by following your heart and sharing your gifts with all whom you meet every day to the best of your ability. It comes from focusing on the good in your life, by laughing a lot, by keeping your mind centered on the beauty of life and away from the demands of your ego, and by being honestly willing to love life and appreciate it every day.

CHAPTER 10

Meditation demystified and made easy

Mingyur Rinpoche – Meditation Master

> *You can apply meditation anywhere: while you are working, in the train, driving a car, having lunch or dinner, while you are singing or while you're watching TV.*

Biography

Born in 1975 in the mountains on the border of Nepal and Tibet, the author is among the generation of Tibetan lamas trained outside of Tibet. At the age of nine, he moved to the hermitage of Nagi Gompa in the foothills of the Kathmandu Valley to study the profound teachings and meditation techniques of the Tibetan Buddhist tradition with his father, Tulku Urgyen Rinpoche, one of the greatest meditation masters of his generation. Then, at the age of 14, Mingyur Rinpoche entered the traditional retreat of three years and three months, becoming the youngest person ever to have done so. Mingyur Rinpoche fuses scientific and spiritual considerations, explaining meditation as a physical as well as a spiritual process. With an infectious joy and insatiable curiosity, Yongey Mingyur weaves together the principles of Tibetan Buddhism, neuroscience and quantum physics in a way that will forever change the way we understand the human experience. Using the basic meditation practices he provides, we can discover the solution to everyday problems, transform obstacles into opportunities and recognize the unlimited potential of our own minds. Having worked with neuroscientists at The Waisman Laboratory for Brain Imaging and Behavior in Madison, Wisconsin, Yongey Mingyur is uniquely qualified to provide fresh insights into new research, which indicates that systematic training in meditation can enhance activity in areas of the brain associated with happiness and compassion. He has also worked with leading physicists to develop a fresh, scientifically based interpretation of the Buddhist understanding of the nature of reality.

Yongey (pronounced Yon-gay) Mingyur Rinpoche is a highly venerated teacher and master of the Karma Kagyu lineage of Tibetan Buddhism. He teaches actively in the West and is known for his remarkable ability to convey the Buddhist teachings in a clear and skillful manner.

How did you start out? What early experiences shaped the person you are today?

I was born in the northern part of Nepal to a wonderful and loving family. My father was a great meditation teacher and I was fortunate to have received a lot of teachings from him. At a young age, I was already very interested in meditation. When I was seven, I began to experience panic attacks and this anxiety followed me like a shadow. At the age of 13, I joined the traditional three-year meditation retreat at Sherab Ling monastery in Northern India. During the first year of the retreat, my panic condition became worse. I was confident that meditation practice could alleviate my panic condition, but I was still too lazy to practice consistently. Then one day, motivated to find relief from my panic attacks, I decided to sit in my room for two days and meditate. During that time I learned to sit with my discomfort. I learned to find the middle way between trying to avoid the discomfort and letting it take me over. I used the sensations related to the panic themselves as the support for my meditation. Eventually, panic became one of my closest friends.

I finished the meditation retreat when I was 17. At the end of that year our retreat master passed away, and it was then that I began to teach. I also joined the traditional "Shedra" (a Tibetan monastic college of higher Buddhist studies) and studied for nine years. In 2001, I started traveling to the East and West sharing my own meditation experience and how my panic problem was my motivation to meditate.

My pa.nic condition helped me to understand that whenever we encounter a problem or obstacle, we can choose how to deal with it. If you challenge your problem too directly (my panic problem, for example) it often becomes an enemy with whom you will constantly have to fight. Similarly, if you put up with the problem, it can become a tyrant that controls your actions and emotions. The best option is to consider your problems as teachers and learn from each difficulty you encounter. This is applicable to any difficulty you may face. I now see my old panic problem as a friend and a wise teacher that reminds me to be who I am. This approach is the basis of my book entitled *The Joy of Living*, which has been translated into 22 languages.

What do you believe is the best way for a person to find their purpose in life?

I believe in helping others. The main purpose of life is to be kind, to help and to contribute to others. This is also beneficial for oneself; it is a win-win situation. If you help others, you are helping yourself. If you harm others, you will harm yourself in a sense. Although you might think it's possible to gain something by harming others, over the long term this will generate problems and you will end up losing. We are all dependent on one another. To be happy, you have to depend on others. If there were no one else in this world, how could you find happiness? There would be nothing to eat, nothing to do, no houses or cars, no money and no friends. Of course you could meditate, but there would be no teachers to teach you how! I believe the main goal of our life is to be kind and care for one another.

What do you believe to be the secret to true happiness?

I believe the secret of happiness is cultivating what I call "inner joy." What is the meaning of inner joy? It is an experience of calm, peace and clarity that doesn't depend on outer circumstances. Inner joy is attained through wisdom that arises from meditation. What is the meaning of wisdom? Wisdom is to see and understand the real nature of the phenomenal world and the real nature of your mind. To realize this wisdom, we must use an effective method such as meditation. Once we have developed awareness and mindfulness through meditation, our minds can become flexible, open, and peaceful.

Even if you're greatly knowledgeable in Buddhist philosophy, but haven't combined that knowledge with the wisdom that arises from meditation, then your learning will be mere words. On the other hand, if you have excellent experience in meditation, but have little understanding of Buddha's teachings, you won't know how to help others. This is why we need to join meditation practice with study.

You have this potential for inner joy within you. Inner joy is a potential in all of us, which we need to recognize. So how do we recognize it? It is through developing wisdom through meditation practice. The meditation method called "Calm Abiding" ("Shamatha" in Sanskrit) enhances the experiences of mindfulness and awareness. Through training in this way, you can experience true happiness and joy, which are independent of outside circumstances. If your happiness is derived from outside circumstances, your emotions will always fluctuate. If you can attain inner joy like this, everything in your life, your family, jobs, and health will benefit.

How would you define genuine success?

It's important to understand the meaning of success. Some people think that dating, having money, fame, or a little peace is being successful. However, I think success is only genuine if it is good for you and others. Everyone should be able to experience peace. How can that come about? We need to ripen the qualities of mind and heart through the development of wisdom, loving kindness, and compassion. Of course this could be difficult, but we all have great potential abiding naturally within us. Although not everyone recognizes it, we have wisdom, loving kindness, and compassion within us. Once you realize these inner qualities, our relationships, family, health, and work will benefit. If you are simply motivated by material gain, in the short term you could be successful, but your emotions will fluctuate with changing external conditions. You might have plenty of money and things, but, you'll always feel busy and restless.

A very rich and famous person once came to me for meditation advice because he wasn't content. He said that money had given him a better life, but not a happier life. If you don't find real happiness, you won't have real success. The meaning of success is to achieve happiness, to achieve inner joy. If your success brings you more suffering, then it's not real success. If you have a lot of stuff, will it necessarily make you content?

In a scientific study, your brain has displayed a variety of mental states through your focus, attention, and meditation. Can you tell us about this experiment?

I went to the University of Wisconsin and under the guidance of Dr Richard J. Davidson I had my brain imaged with FMRI (functional magnetic-resonance imaging) technology.

They invited me and other meditation practitioners (meaning those who have meditated for at least 10,000 hours) to take part in the experiment. The researchers monitored our brain activity before and during meditation. They observed remarkable changes in brain activity during the experiment. FMRI is like a movie that allows you to observe neurons and the various activities of the brain. I sat inside a big machine for anywhere between 1 to 1.5 hours per session. The researchers put many electrical sensors on my head. In that experiment, I was asked to meditate using three meditation techniques: 1. open presence; 2. focusing on an object; and 3. unconditional loving kindness and compassion.

While I was meditating in these ways they had me listen to various frightening noises including a girl screaming and a baby crying. The scientists observed a variety of changes in brain function during the experiment. The changes were so dramatic that they assumed that the machines were malfunctioning. Over time they realized that the changes in brain function were, in fact, the result of the meditation. They learned that positive states of mind are marked by high activity in the left frontal area of the brain. They observed dramatic changes in what they now call "the area of happiness". This was very exciting news and led to a lot of discussion with the scientists. They have been able to verify through the testing that meditation really is extremely beneficial. There are three important points:

The brain demonstrates "Neuronal Plasticity", meaning our brain is capable of change. Ten years ago neuroscientists didn't believe that the brain was capable of change. Now we know that even if you're born unhappy it's possible to become happy.

The best way to effect this change is through daily meditation practice.

Positive change on our emotions is good for our heart and, our immune system, and helps to reduce stress levels.

What, exactly, did you do to achieve a happy and peaceful state of mind? What can an average person learn from this?

I use my problems and difficulties as a motivation to practice. In this way, my mind becomes more peaceful and stable. Otherwise, if you think that suffering is something to avoid, and that happiness is to be attained from somewhere else, your experience will forever go up and down like the stock market. I use whatever arises as a support for my meditation practice. This is how I used my panic experiences as a support for my practice.

Most people think happiness is dependent on outer conditions such as wealth or fame. In reality, happiness is within you. With meditation, we need to combine awareness with wisdom. You can say there are two steps, applying the right method, and developing wisdom. To develop wisdom, you need to change your perception. Training in awareness and mindfulness through meditation practice is like physical exercise. You go to the gym and develop muscles and, as a reward, you'll be healthier. Similarly, you need mental exercise to develop mental muscles. Meditation is like a mental workout. Everyone can do this.

Even a little bit of meditation can help a lot. Some universities have studied beginning meditators. These meditators practiced everyday for one hour for eight consecutive weeks. After eight weeks, the students showed remarkable brain development and were able to gain better control of their emotions.

You have traveled quite extensively across the East and West. What is a common problem contributing to people's lack of fulfillment in life?

The most common problem is people's never-ending expectations. Say you earn $1000. It may be plenty to live on, but you want more. When you make $10,000, you wish you could make $100,000. There is always the expectation of wanting more and more.

I once met a man who lived in a cave in Brazil. He didn't have a lot of food, just wild bananas and fruit. However, he was an excellent meditator and was very happy living in a cave and sailing in the ocean. He is happy because he's satisfied. On the other hand, some rich and famous people I've met aren't satisfied with their lives. They're unhappy because of their expectations. We need to strike a balance. Of course we need a goal, but we should focus more on the motivation behind what we do than the result. It's good to try to accomplish what we want, but we shouldn't be too tied up in the goal. You need to accept your situation, because you're not going to succeed all the time.

How can we attain lasting happiness?

Attaining lasting happiness depends on you. If you have "inner joy" then your happiness is unshakable. However, if you depend on outside circumstances for your happiness, you will never achieve real happiness. I often ask my students whether they can find one object that they all agree is precious. Some think that one thing is precious, while others disagree. They can't find any one thing that everyone considers to be precious: diamonds, gold, fortune, fame, or anything else. Keep in mind that real happiness and joy is within you. If you can come to the realization of what that means, then that is wisdom. To develop this wisdom, you need to apply mindfulness and awareness. In this way, you can attain lasting happiness.

What is temporal, as distinct from permanent, happiness? How can we attain the latter state?

If you look to outside circumstances to find happiness, you will always be disappointed. Outside circumstances are impermanent, so any happiness derived there will be similarly impermanent. Lasting happiness comes from within you. When you discover the nature of your mind, you discover the joy that is independent of external circumstances. Mind's essence is calm and clear by nature. This is experienced as joy, or unshakable happiness. This is the central message of the Buddha, that mind's abiding nature is calm, clear, and compassionate. When monkey mind is tamed and mind's nature is allowed to shine through, this is what we discover.

You have worked extensively with some of the world's leading neuroscientists, biologists, and psychologists. Does scientific research show how and why Buddhist-based teaching works?

The teachings and techniques of Buddhism work through changing the quality and flexibility of the brain. Specifically, the practices of mindfulness, along with loving kindness and compassion can transform our minds and our perception. This change in perception allows us to experience natural and unchanging happiness.

How does modern science parallel Buddhist teaching? How can we benefit from these findings at a practical level?

Modern science and the Buddha's teaching on the "science" of mind both look to understand the genuine nature of phenomena. Both science and the Buddha's teaching describe a world that, while it appears and functions, when examined is seen to be without substance: it is seen to be impermanent and insubstantial. Suffering is caused by mistaking that which is without essence (the appearances of this world and our sense of "me"), to be real and permanent. Some people can experience this truth through the teachings and practice of Buddhism, but others need this truth to be confirmed by scientific theory and method. In these times, it seems scientific discoveries shape a culture's beliefs and assumptions. To the degree that the modern findings of science can be joined with ancient teachings of the Buddha, people can be profoundly inspired and benefited.

Recently, Western science has been able to validate many of the Buddha's teachings on the nature of reality through scientific method. The Buddha's emphasis on compassion and altruism helps us to skillfully use these insights to relieve the suffering of beings.

An understanding of the insubstantial and impermanent nature of reality can help us to decrease our grasping and fixation on the world. With less grasping, peace and well being are close at hand. Buddhist principles can bring a sense of heart to the insights of science.

Can I practice Buddhist teaching even if I'm not a Buddhist and what are the immediate benefits?

Yes of course. The Buddha's teachings and methods are beneficial regardless of religious affiliation. The key practices that the Buddha taught are the training of mind through the meditation of calm abiding, and the development of kindness and compassion for all beings. Just the desire and early training in these qualities bring tremendous benefit. It also suffuses our lives with a sense of meaning. In order to deepen this training, it's also helpful to study a little of the Buddha's teachings on impermanence, the fact that actions have results (karma) and the nature of phenomena as being "empty of self".

It has been said that by changing the direction of the mind, we can change the quality of everything we experience. What are this adage's daily applications?

The mind is like a king and your body and actions are like the followers. In our life there is happiness and unhappiness. But, what is happiness and what is unhappiness anyway? It depends on your state of mind and what you are thinking.

We always follow the lead of mind. For example, if your family doctor advises you to go to the sauna more often to help your immune system, then you would go to the sauna and enjoy it, despite the fact that you normally hate the heat. You might even pay a lot and make special time in your busy schedule in order to go to the sauna. Or, even though strong exercise is difficult, if you decide to do it in order to experience the result of having a healthy body, you'll begin to enjoy the exertion. This is an example of how your outlook changes the quality of your experience.

The mind determines the experience of happiness or unhappiness. The mind is powerful, so you have the choice of changing your experience from negative to positive. Because of this you can develop happiness, wisdom, compassion, love and kindness. How do we do that? It is through training in wisdom and meditation as I've mentioned before.

Please explain the concept of dualistic consciousness; how do we break free from this cycle?

Dualistic perception is a mistaken perception of a solid, truly existing object being perceived by a solid, truly existing self. This mistaken perception is the basis for all of our confusion and struggle. To break free of this cycle of dualistic perception, we need to recognize that, in fact, self and other are both impermanent and hence imaginary. In order for understanding to become our experience, we need to recognize the true nature of mind, which sees itself and the world as they truly are, beyond duality. This is not a concept, but a direct experience born of meditation. Our mind is fundamentally beyond duality. It is fundamentally beyond concept. If you recognize this, you can break free from dualistic perception. We can realize this by developing wisdom through meditation practice.

What is meditation, and what are the benefits of practicing for today's world?

Meditation in Tibetan is called "Gom." Gom means "to become familiar" with positive experiences such as peace, calm, and clarity. The key point of meditation is to apply awareness and mindfulness.

These are the main points of meditation and there are two basic types:

1) "Ordinary awareness" is when you are aware of normal happenings around you. This is common to everyone.

2) "Meditative awareness" is different from ordinary awareness.

Ordinary awareness faces inwards, but it isn't aware of its own awareness. Meditative awareness faces inward but that awareness is recognized. You are aware that you are aware. So what is the meaning of facing inward? For example, when you listen to a sound, you normally just hear the sound.

But for a meditator, you would at the same time be aware of how your body hears and responds to the sound. You would be alert to your actions, behaviors, thoughts and emotions

Awareness is always present behind thoughts, and emotions. There is no judgment here. What do I mean? For example, if you use sound as part of your meditation, the sound can be labeled as pleasant or unpleasant. In meditation, you don't attach yourself to the sound. You simply listen and hear the sound. The important thing is to develop mindfulness and awareness. In normal circumstances, we don't do that.

Some people equate the nature of mind with a monkey. What do you have to say about this?

It's not the nature of the mind that is equated with a monkey; it is the character or behavior of the mind. They are different. The mind itself is pure, good, and amazing. However, it can behave strangely sometimes. If you set a monkey free in a grocery store, it will be overjoyed and jump everywhere, and end up making a mess in the store. This is its natural behavior. Our mind is like that monkey. It always ends up making trouble. If there is no problem, monkey mind tries to mess things up and create new problems. If there's a big problem, then monkey mind is happy. If there's no problem, then monkey mind looks for a problem and turns a small obstacle into a big problem. This is what a monkey does.

There are many types of meditation. How can a person get started and know what is the best method?

From my own experience, there are two types of meditations that are best for beginners. The first is called "Shamatha without an object," the art of relaxing your body and mind (with no special object). The second type of meditation uses various objects as support. There are three objects that are very important for beginners.

    a)   The use of "sounds" – close your eyes, relax your body, and listen to the sound. Simply be aware of the sound. Don't focus too much on the sound, just be aware of it. Open your ears and listen to the sound. It doesn't matter what kind of sound it is. You can even change your focus from one sound to another sound, as long as you can maintain mindfulness.

However, don't focus on too many sounds as you may get confused as to which sound to use. You can choose a sound that is clear for you. You won't be able to maintain mindfulness of the sound for long. Just meditate for five minutes. After that you can take a break for a while and start again.

b) In the same way, you can use the sensations and movement of the body as the support for your mindfulness.

c) Finally, you can use your speech as the support for your meditation. You can repeat "OM AH HUNG." These are what Buddhists refer to as the three enlightened syllables. "OM" is enlightened body, "AH" is enlightened speech and "HUNG" is enlightened mind. Alternatively, you can use words like "compassion, compassion, compassion." If you follow a different tradition or religion you can say short and simple prayers from those traditions. Repeat them again and again in your mind. For example, if you repeat "OM AH HUNG," relax your body and keep your spine straight. Repeat the words mentally. If, other thoughts arise, like "OM – What should I do tomorrow? AH – I'm hungry, HUNG – I'm tired," that's OK, just relax and come back to "OM AH HUNG'" again and again. Don't attempt to control or block your thoughts.

If you become distracted, just notice it and return to the repetition.

What benefits can we expect if the mind becomes restful and clear?

A rested and clear mind is incredibly beneficial. For example, if your mind is restful and clear, then it's good for your body. Scient.5ific research shows that meditation boosts your immune system. Because your mind controls your life, meditation helps all aspects of your experience. If your mind becomes clear and calm, you can control how you think and perceive. A clear mind helps you in your education, in your work and in your relationships with others.

If your mind is clouded by your thoughts and emotions, you will have difficulty learning. It's like a computer with a full hard drive—there's no room for more information. In the same way, if your mind is clear and peaceful, it will be receptive and fresh. A clear mind is also more balanced and joyful.

To begin meditation, is it better to have long, or short and frequent sessions?

If you just started practicing meditation, short sessions are better. For example, you can set a goal. Let's say you want to meditate for 15 minutes. During these 15 minutes, you should apply the technique for a short time, take a break and apply the technique again. Why? Your mind cannot rest on the meditation for more than a short time in the beginning. In only a second or two you will lose that meditation, so shorter and more frequent sessions are better. It could be as short as two to three seconds, which you repeat many times in one minute.

You can begin with repeating 5 to 15 times. When you can rest for your mind for longer periods, you can meditate for two to three hours and still be comfortable.

Short periods of meditation are good for keeping your mind fresh. If you do it many times, it develops your meditation experience. Your mind will be clearer and stronger. You can apply meditation anywhere: while you are working, in the train, driving a car, having lunch or dinner, while you are singing or while you're watching TV. Next time when you queue up for a train ticket, just try to meditate and practice. "Short time, many times" is very important.

Most people are occupied with many commitments in their life, such as their job and family. How can they find time for, and what is the best time for meditation?

One of the best times for meditation is in the early morning. If you have a good rest in the night, your mind should be quite clear when you wake up in the morning. Start with 10 to 15 minutes of meditation. Beyond that you don't need to worry too much about having enough time to meditate. Meditation as I've described it can be done at any time and anywhere. So don't worry about having to fit meditation in your busy schedule.

When resting the mind, it seems that the harder we try the more active the mind becomes. How can we overcome this?

You have to know that the important point of meditation is to follow the nature of mind. For example, when listening to a sound, you simply have to be aware that you're listening. Just be aware that you're listening to a sound. That's it. If you focus too hard, meditation becomes difficult. Simply note that you're attending to a sound.

How can we use our life's every encounter and experience as a lesson?

This is a good question. The point here is that life is very colorful and interesting. Of course there is suffering, happiness, change, and uncertainty. We can learn a tremendous amount from our troubles and difficulties. Difficulties and obstacles are one of our best teachers.

I had a lot of trouble with panic attacks when I was young. I'm grateful for those experiences. One of the reasons I'm teaching and sharing my experience today is because of those panic attacks and the incentive they gave me to find relief. If you're curious about your life, then everything becomes a lesson. Everything can contribute to your happiness.

About Joseph

Joseph Rodarick Law is an entrepreneur, investor, bestselling author, speaker and philanthropist.

He is the Chairman and CEO of J Rodarick Corporation, a consulting and corporate advisory firm serving private and public companies in corporate finance transactions, including advice on implementation of mergers and acquisitions, trade sales, private equity transactions and stock exchange listings across Australia, Hong Kong, China, South East Asia, India, the United States and Europe.

Joseph speaks regularly at international conferences and Fortune 500 companies including L'Oreal, Optus, Johnson & Johnson, JP Morgan, as well as universities including University of Sydney and University of Wollongong. He has interviewed heads of states, billionaires, CEOs, bestselling authors, celebrities, a Nobel prize laureate and people from all walks of life.

Joseph has been interviewed by international media, including AFR, Sky News, the Financial Times and The Wall Street Journal, and by such Chinese media as CCTV, China Business News, China Securities Journal and Xinhua News Agency.

Joseph sits on the advisory board of the Australia-China Relations Institute, headed by former Foreign Minister of Australia, Honorable Bob Carr. He was nominated by US Ambassador Hugo Llorens as the Young Global Leader of the World Economic Forum.

Joseph travels extensively around the world and is the co-founder of JC Happiness Charity Foundation.

You can find him at www.josephrodaricklaw.com.

UK £12.99
US $22.99